John Paul II
Speaks to Youth
at World Youth Day

John Paul II
Speaks to Youth
at World Youth Day

Edited and Illustrated
by
Catholic News Service

Ignatius Press   San Francisco
Catholic News Service   Washington, D.C.

General Editor: Thomas N. Lorsung, director and editor-in-chief, Catholic News Service
Photo Editor: Barbara Stephenson, photos and graphics manager, Catholic News Service
Writer for chapters one and five: Julie Asher
Writer for chapters two through four and six through eleven: Carol Zimmermann
Photo coordinator, Denver: Joanne Asher
Photo researchers: Sarah Davis in Washington; Kate Marcelin-Rice in Rome
With the collaboration of: Mark Lombard, Mary Bozzonetti, James M. Lackey, David Gibson, Juli Peters Delong, Joseph Larson, Pamela Risik, Agostino Bono, John Thavis, Cindy Wooden, Bill Pritchard, Barb Fraze, Nancy Frazier O'Brien, Jerry Filteau, Patricia Zapor, Mark Pattison, Carl Eifert, Mary Esslinger, Lou Panarale, Carole Greene, Bessie Briscoe, Gloria T. Moore, Marie Williams, Randy Hall, Regina Edwards, Caole Lowry and Terrell Sims.

Design: Preston Bautista
Typography: Giraffe-x

Cover photography: Arturo Mari
Cover design: Roxanne Mei Lum

ISBN 0–89870–479–0 (HB)
ISBN 0–89870–480–4 (SB)

Library of Congress catalogue number 93-61455

Printed in the United States of America

Contents

Message from the Delegates of the Fourth International Youth Forum

We come from all corners of the earth; from the Middle East to Europe, from Africa to Asia, from Australia to the Americas. We are the delegates from the fourth International Youth Forum, a gathering of 270 young adults. We have come to Denver to deepen our understanding of what it means to be ``born to a new life in Jesus Christ.'' We gain strength from the Virgin Mary, the first to experience the new life of Jesus Christ. Today, we wish to speak to the youth of the world not about problems, despair, and hatred, but about possibilities, hope, and love.

Many of us have brought to this forum not only our youthfulness and faith, but also pain of war, disunity, the divisiveness of racism, the indifference of materialism, and the perils of poverty. We could wallow in the complexities and the enormities of these problems. On the one hand we could choose the easy way out and say and do nothing about them. On the other hand we could make our voice ring out with strength, roll up our sleeves and work for change. We know the World Youth Day participants have embraced the latter. Through dialogue, prayer, and reflecting on God's word we have witnessed a communion with God, a true sense of community, and a commitment to the Church as an anticipation of the kingdom of God. The International Youth Forum has been for us an excellent opportunity for dialogue and discussion, and the attentiveness of the bishops and pastors of the Church has been a great joy.

We recognize that in the Church we are born in faith and continue to be revived. We ask the pastors to continue to help us discover our vocation, our direction in society and in the Church, by giving us the formation we need as young Christians. The new catechism, which we have received with great happiness, together with the free expression of our youthfulness will be the most valuable instrument to grow in faith. We know this formation comes not only through words and teachings, but also through the example of living Christ's life; formation does not come only through the Church's structure, but also through the testimony of a holy life.

We recognize that united with our brothers and sisters we are the Church of today and the Church of tomorrow. We share with believers and nonbelievers alike a thirst for truth, a hunger for solidarity, and a desire for self-giving. As youth we tend to be demanding, critical, and inquisitive. We do not ask the young people to abandon their uncertainties, questions, or criticisms. Rather we ask all those who call themselves Christians to allow themselves to be guided by grace to encounter Christ in the Church, through the sacraments, prayer, and the reception of the word. With the help of these means we strive to live mercy and solidarity and thus always be open to our neighbors. We are confident that the first place where this spirit can be lived, experienced, and felt is through the family.

From our Christian experience, we want to share with all the world's youth our desire to build a new society, a society of love. We strive to develop our personal gifts to the best of our ability so as to better serve society. We strive to serve in particular, the weakest, the poorest, and the most vulnerable among us. To make this a reality we need to walk together, hand in hand, with all the youth and all the people of the world who love life.

We thank Pope John Paul II, Peter's successor, for his encouragement and we pledge to him to be the new evangelizers and the living stones of the Church. We are convinced of one thing: In Christ we can change the world. But before we can change the world each one of us has to change his heart through humility.

Foreword

Pope John Paul II loves young people. And the feeling is mutual.

This book celebrates that love in words and photos. It's about World Youth Day, but it's a bigger story than that.

The youths of World Youth Day are the Church of today and of tomorrow. They have their ups and their downs, their doubts and their delights.

But don't we all?

The message of the book is the message of the Holy Father as he visits his family's youngest and most enthusiastic members: Life in the Church is life in Christ.

The theme of World Youth Day from its earliest days says it all: ``I came so that they might have life and have it more abundantly." (John 10:10)

May you as a reader be inspired to experience this life more fully because of what you see in these pages. If you were among the thousands who attended these events, may the words and photos recapture and enhance your precious memories!

Thomas N. Lorsung
Director and editor in chief
Catholic News Service

CHAPTER 1

The Pope and Youth: A Love Story

Pope John Paul II and the world's youth—the combination has always seemed natural, almost magical, even from the first hours of his pontificate. At his inauguration ceremonies on October 22, 1978, he closed with a special greeting to youth: "You are the future of the world, you are the hope of the Church, you are my hope."

Young people have seemed ever present, whether the pope was participating in the international World Youth Day observances, attending other youth gatherings in Italy or elsewhere, greeting groups at the Vatican and Castel Gandolfo or taking time out for them during many of his fifty-eight pastoral trips outside Italy.

He has always made a point, he says, to see young people on his trips, because "the future of the world shines in your eyes."

The visits have seemed a balm, an antidote to the heavy workload of the Church's leader. He lights up in the presence of young people. In fact, he seems to get younger.

"He looks younger and younger every day you are here," Cardinal Agostino Casaroli, then Vatican Secretary of State, told a group of British young people at a Holy Year event in 1984. "If you stay here much longer, we'll have a pope who looks like a young Christian."

With a hearty, athletic approach to life and a youthful vigor, the pope has energized the Catholic Church in a way his predecessors did not. But it has also been the vigor of the world's young people that has seemed so often to energize him.

In a spontaneous moment in Los Angeles in 1987, the pope jumped down from a stage to approach Tony Melendez, a twenty-five-year-old armless guitar player who had just performed for him. Breaking from the script, he went to Melendez to embrace him and kiss him on the cheek.

Growing Up

Even as a young parish priest, the future pope devoted much of his time to young people—teaching religion, playing soccer and leading philosophical discussions.

His own childhood and youth had been marked by emotional trauma. Karol Jozef Wojtyla was born May 18, 1920, in Wadowice, a small town near Krakow in southern Poland. When he was nine, his mother died. Three years later, he lost his only brother, Edmund, to scarlet fever. When Wojtyla was twenty, his father died. Friends said he knelt for twelve hours in prayer and sorrow at the bedside of the man who had been his closest companion and strongest influence. Added to the losses of the three people closest to him were the hardships placed on Wojtyla by the political situation that existed during his youth.

Remembered in high school as a bright,

Opposite page: In a historic moment, April, 1993, the Holy Father comes to the children of Albania. Until just recently Albania had been an officially "atheistic state" where the Church had been brutally persecuted and where even to give a child a Christian name had been considered a crime.

Father Wojtyla, an avid athlete, takes a break to read in his kayak in 1955, three years before he became a bishop.

athletic young man with a contemplative side, Wojtyla excelled in religion, philosophy and languages. He also worked to help support his father. In 1938, he began studies for a philosophy degree at the University of Krakow, joining speech and drama clubs and writing his own poetry.

The Nazi blitzkrieg of Poland on September 1, 1939, left the country in ruins and opened a new chapter in Wojtyla's life. During the German occupation, he helped set up an underground university and the clandestine Rhapsodic Theatre. At the same time he found work in a stone quarry and a chemical factory—experiences he later analyzed in poems and papal writings.

> **His students gave him the nickname "the eternal teenager."**

"Even as a boy he was exceptional," said Rafat Tatka, a neighbor from the pope's hometown of Wadowice, who knew the young Wojtyla as "Lolek," which might be translated as "Chuck."

Jerzy Kluger, a Jewish boyhood friend of Lolek, recalled him as a defender of local Jews even as anti-Semitism began to surface before World War II. He told the story of a woman who, finding the two young friends chatting in the Wadowice cathedral one day, questioned the presence of the Jewish boy in the church. Wojtyla laughed in response and asked, "Aren't we all God's children?"

Kluger said of his friend, "He was first in school, in the theatre, in everything. If he had gone to General Motors, he would have become president."

Wojtyla had a much higher calling, however. He entered Krakow's clandestine theological seminary in 1942 and was ordained in Krakow on November 1, 1946. He then was sent to Rome for studies. In 1948 he received a doctorate in ethics from Rome's Angelicum University.

The Outdoor Sportsman

Back in Poland, he first served in the rural village of Niegowic and then was sent to St. Florian Parish in Krakow. There he always made time for the youth of the parish, managing to squeeze in games of soccer between preaching and teaching, visiting parishioners and performing baptisms and marriages.

Then he took a partial sabbatical to earn a doctoral degree in moral theology. In 1953, he began lecturing at Lublin University. There his students gave him the nickname "the eternal teenager." The energetic priest would take them hiking, canoeing and camping. Together they would swim, sing, talk

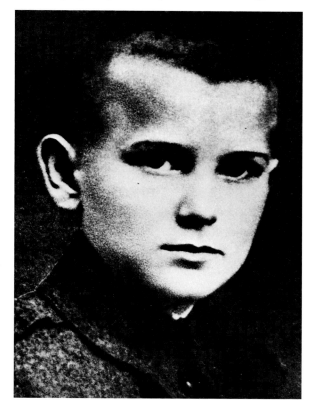

Young Karol Josef Wojtyla dressed in his school uniform at age 12. The name "Karol" is the Polish equivalent of the name "Charles." As a boy, young Karol had the nickname "Lolek," which we would translate as "Chuck" in English.

> **Even as a young parish priest, the future pope devoted much of his time to young people.**

and pray. And he always celebrated Mass for them.

The road to his pontificate began when he was named a bishop in 1958, Poland's youngest bishop. The announcement of his appointment caught up with him while he was canoeing with friends. He traveled to Warsaw to receive the news formally, but he was back on the water the same day.

Close To Youth

The future pope rose quickly through the ranks, becoming an archbishop in 1964. In 1967 Pope Paul VI named him a cardinal—the second-youngest in the Church. Despite his rapid ecclesiastical ascent, Cardinal Wojtyla remained a virtual unknown to many in the Church—until the evening of October 16, 1978, when his election as pope was announced to some two hundred thousand people gathered in St. Peter's Square and to the world at large.

The following day, one of his countrymen, Bishop Boleslaw Dabrowski, then Secretary General of the Polish bishops' conference, remarked that the Church's new leader "works like an ox, sleeps very little and is very open, especially to youth." So began a pontificate remarkable in many ways, not in small part because of his numerous encounters with young people. The pontiff has sung with them, prayed with them, talked to them—whether at the World Youth Day celebration in Argentina, Spain, Poland or the United States, at a racecourse in Ireland, a jail in Rome, a stadium in Paris, an arena in Tokyo, the Olympic Stadium in Montreal, the Superdome in New Orleans or a rally in Lusaka, Zambia. "Awesome" is how many young people have described the experience of being with the pope. "It was neat." "It was so moving." "A real spiritual high." In Sydney, Australia, he was dubbed "The Dancing Pope" when he kicked up his heels to pop music. During one visit to a Rome parish, he gave basketball tips to some youngsters gathered in a nearby schoolyard.

He has even spent time with young people on his birthday. When he turned sixty-five, he ended a full day of celebrating at a meeting with about thirty thousand young people in French-speaking Namur, Belgium. "Your presence here is for me like a wonderful birthday present," he said.

His message has always been that young people are the hope of the world and should try to promote love and peace and make a difference in a world beset by oppression, civil wars, indifference, greed, consumerism and materialism. And, he has urged, they need to work for the good of the Church.

Encouraging Greatness

He has often matched the symbolism in his message to the setting. In greeting young campers at Castel Gandolfo one summer, Pope John Paul II said: "The Church must build herself up everywhere, following the example of our Lord and the inspiration of the Holy Spirit. I am convinced, also from personal experience, that the growth and development of the Church can be accomplished very well in a camp."

He has asked young people to lead lives of charity and of chastity, saving sex for marriage. He has also challenged some among them to "put yourselves in the front line" as priests, religious and missionaries.

But he has listened to young people, too. Question-and-answer periods have often been included in his meetings with young people.

The pope-to-be enjoys a visit with Polish schoolchildren.

During his stop in Los Angeles on a visit to the United States, the pontiff fielded questions in a teleconference at the Universal Amphitheater. Attended by sixty-two hundred local teenagers, the event included a hook-up to teens in Denver, St. Louis and Portland, Oregon. Pope John Paul II

Smooth! Bishop Wojtyla lathers up for an outdoor shave during a 1959 mountain climbing expedition.

answered questions about why he travels, about his own youth and about the pressures he faces.

He has always urged young people to choose whatever promotes life and goodness in society, to stand up against violence and evil, to seek to bring peace and hope. In a 1984 event, during the closing Mass of the Holy Year of Redemption, 250,000 young people filled St. Peter's Square in the Vatican. It was the biggest turnout there since the funeral of Paul VI and the inauguration of two pontiffs in 1978.

"Who says the youth of today have lost their values?" the pope said, upon seeing the crowd. He assured them that they were important for the future of the Church, and he urged them to be messengers of peace to a suffering world.

"In a very real sense, the twenty-first century, which is rapidly approaching, belongs to you. I ask you, therefore, to think carefully about the

choices in life which you have to make," the pope told them. Carrying palms, some more than six feet tall, the young people walked to St. Peter's Square from two different points in Rome. Visibly moved by the crowd, the pope praised the young people for their religious spirit. "What a marvelous spectacle this assembly makes in the setting of this square," the pope said.

> **"In a very real sense, the twenty-first century…belongs to you. I ask you, therefore, to think carefully about the choices in life which you have to make."**

How World Youth Day Got Started

In 1985 he issued a fifteen-thousand-word apostolic letter specifically addressed to the world's youth. In it, Pope John Paul II called on them to use their strength, "not for the struggle of one against another," but for "the struggle against evil." He said "the real evil" was everything that offends God: injustice, exploitation, falsehood, deceit, "everything that profanes human society and human relationships" and "every crime against life."

Later that year the pope announced his desire for a youth day observance to celebrate the faith of young Catholics worldwide. His announcement came in an address at the end of 1985, the United Nations' International Youth Year.

In January 1986, the Pontifical Council for the Laity, charged with overseeing the celebrations, released details on the annual event, to take place every Palm Sunday. The laity council "warmly invited" bishops throughout the world to put the event on their calendars. For the first celebration, in 1986, bishops were urged to plan youth events in their dioceses.

The pope that year addressed his Palm Sunday homily to the world's youth, challenging them to work and pray for world peace. "In this way," he said, "a great moral force will grow in the world so threatened by the arms race, hate, terrorism and the violation of human rights, especially the right to life from the moment of conception until death."

That first Vatican observance set in motion an international youth event, now held every other year, in which the pope himself participates. He also has issued an annual message for each World Youth Day.

Past To Present

For the 1987 World Youth Day in Buenos Aires, Argentina—the first youth day held outside the Vatican—he called on the world's young people to build a "civilization of love."

The pope arrived in Buenos Aires to find a crowd of about four hundred thousand, comprised mostly of Argentineans. Youth delegations also attended from other Latin American countries, Europe, Africa and the United States.

The pope told the young people not to let their enthusiasm fade. He also explained that he had picked Palm Sunday as World Youth Day to emphasize the need for permanent enthusiasm and commitment by Christians.

"Palm Sunday introduces us to all the events of Holy Week and the total mystery of Jesus Christ. It introduces us to his giving until death on the Cross because of obedience to the Father," the pope said.

In 1989 the pope went "to the end of the earth" to encourage youth to build a better world and fortify their spiritual lives. This trip was to the World Youth Day in Santiago de Compostela, twenty miles from the Atlantic Ocean in the northwest corner of Spain. During the centuries when the coast of Europe was the end of the known world, Santiago de Compostela was the last major city before reaching the sea—thus the "title."

In his message for that World Youth Day, the pope stressed that the "world of today is a great mission land." "Everywhere today neopaganism and the process of secularization present a great challenge to the message of the Gospel," he said. The Church needs "apostles who are young and courageous" to take advantage of the "new open-

Dig the shades! Bishop Wojtyla visits the Parthenon in Athens in 1963, on his way to the Holy Land.

ings" for evangelization, he said.

The next international youth day was held in 1991 in Czestochowa, Poland, at the Shrine of Our Lady of Czestochowa, Poland's most important pilgrimage center. In his message for the event, the pope encouraged growing contacts between young people of the East and the West. Because of the democratic reforms sweeping through many of the former Communist-controlled countries, this marked the first time many young people from Eastern European nations would be allowed to attend a Church-sponsored international meeting.

Once in his homeland, Pope John Paul II

Though much has changed in the life of the pope, some things haven't changed at all — like his love for young people. Audience members greet the pope during a teleconference with youth in Los Angeles in 1987.

told a gathering of more than one million people to seize the moment, now that ideological barriers were down, to reconstruct their personal and national lives. "Become builders of a new world: a different world, founded on truth, justice, solidarity and love."

The crowd of young people included about seventy thousand from the Soviet Union. It was the first time the Soviet government had allowed young people to leave the country to participate in the Catholic youth rally. "The Church in Europe can breathe freely now with both her lungs," the pope said.

Two years later the pope was bound for Denver.

On April 12, 1992, the pontiff announced the city that would host the 1993 World Youth Day, ending weeks of speculation. He had had to pick from three finalists—Denver, Minneapolis-St. Paul and Buffalo, New York.

"I have chosen the city of Denver in the famous Rocky Mountains and in the state of Colorado, which has never been included in my previous apostolic trips," the pope said. The theme, he said, would be the life-giving power of the Christian vision.

"In the midst of great historic changes, faced with epochal breakdowns and grave new uncertainties, there is so much need for your emerging strength," he told his young listeners.

From then on, "Denver" was on the pope's lips whenever he met young people. He made it clear he wanted young people to join him in the Mile High City, at the base of "the famous Rocky Mountains," for World Youth Day 1993.

> **"Become builders of a new world: a different world, founded on truth, justice, solidarity and love."**

CHAPTER 2

A Million Voices Call His Name

Hundreds of thousands of young people from around the world literally took the Gospel message to the streets when they met in Buenos Aires, the bustling capital of Argentina, on April 11-12, 1987.

The teenagers and young adults, primarily from Latin America, had not come to the popular city merely for a spring break; instead, they came together to pray and sing and to meet a man they loved—Pope John Paul II. This gathering of young people to meet the pontiff, who had long since passed his teenage years, was starting to become a lively tradition.

"In the capital of the Republic of Argentina, we are united in spirit with St. Peter's Basilica in Rome...where it was the Lord's wish that this youth celebration should be born," the pope told the crowd, reported to be between four hundred thousand and one million young people.

Although the pope was in Argentina as part of his thirteen-day visit to Latin America, it was no coincidence that he chose to address the teens and young adults, who filled twenty blocks of the world's widest street, during an evening prayer vigil and Mass on Palm Sunday. Palm Sunday was the day he had chosen in 1985 for the official celebration of World Youth Day, and it was also the day on which the pope had met with the first two international youth assemblies in 1984 and 1985. At both of these international gatherings, the Holy Father encouraged young people to work for peace.

And so, on this Palm Sunday in the warmth of Buenos Aires, it did not seem unusual for the leader of the Catholic Church to be talking with

To look around and see hundreds of thousands of teens and young adults praying and singing not only helped participants in their understanding of the Church, but it also showed those who watched the events on television "a fresh, different face of the Church." Here, during the Palm Sunday Mass Procession, delegates carry crosses representing the Church around the globe.

hundreds of thousands of young people once again. Fittingly, he reiterated his call for them to be peacemakers. "Be witnesses to the love of Christ, sowers of hope and builders of peace," he told the exuberant, cheering crowd.

Opposite page: "Be witness to the love of Christ, sowers of hope and builders of peace," Pope John Paul II told an exuberant, cheering crowd of between 400,000 to 1,000,000 young people on the world's widest street in Buenos Aires, Argentina, at World Youth Day '87.

Overcoming Painful Experience

The pope's message had particular meaning in light of Argentina's recent history. During the 1970s and 1980s, nine thousand people had disappeared in the country's war between security forces and guerrillas. A war with Britain over the Falkland (Malvinas) Islands in 1982 had also taken hundreds of young lives.

"I know you are determined to overcome the recent painful experiences of your country," the pope said during the prayer vigil. Departing from his prepared text, he added: "May you never again have kidnapped or displaced persons. May you no longer have a place for hate and violence, and may the dignity of the person always be respected."

Although the pope had already been in Argentina for six days, his first public mention of the country's political situation came when he met with the young people. Nieves Tapia, an Argentinean organizer of World Youth Day 1987, said the pope's strong stance against human rights violations was particularly appropriate since Argentina was only in its third year of democracy.

A Volatile Situation

The unrest in the South American country was not just past history, however; some of the World Youth Day participants sensed political instability as soon as they arrived in the Buenos Aires airport. "There was an underlying volatile situation that was very much a part of the environment," said Ellen Dermody, who attended the event with a

Cruising around in the "Popemobile". Pope John Paul II waves to the crowd during the 1987 Palm Sunday Procession. Although the pope had already been in Argentina for six days, he publicly addressed the country's tense political situation only when he met with the young people. He condemned human rights violations and urged the teens and young adults to be "free from so many slaveries such as sexual disorders, drugs, violence and the desire for power," and he implored them to make personal commitments to build "a nation of brothers."

"The pope had been so tired because the day before he met the young people he had visited 10 cities," said Nieves Tapia, an Argentinian organizer of World Youth Day '87, "but during the youth meeting he was so happy and he became more relaxed." Here a young man greets the Holy Father.

group from the Washington Archdiocese. The feeling was more than intuition, for only days after the youth festivities were over, there was an attempted military coup against the president of Argentina.

While talking to the young people, the pope condemned injustices within the country, but he also spoke out against the evils of today's world as a whole. He urged the teens and young adults to be "free from so many slaveries such as sexual disorders, drugs, violence and the desire for power," and he implored them to make personal commitments to build "a nation of brothers."

"The pope tells you what he feels; he is honest," said Bienvenido Martinez, who attended the rally with the Washington delegation. Frequent

shouts of "El Papa, El Papa!" were eloquent proof that the crowd found the pontiff's straightforwardness appealing.

They also, however, gave him their full attention when he spoke. "It was amazing that one million people could be silent while the pope talked," said Alice Redding, who chaperoned a group from the diocese of Harrisburg, Pennsylvania. "You could just see the respect and love between

> **Frequent shouts of "El Papa, El Papa!" were eloquent proof that the crowd found the pontiff's straightforwardness appealing.**

young people and the pope. He was very complimentary to the young people and also challenging," telling them to use their faith in service to others, she said. "The pope seemed to be very much aware of the problems facing young people. From the little bit I could understand (in Spanish), he seemed to have high hopes for them."

Teenagers and young adults in the crowd strained to see Pope John Paul II, but the distance between themselves and the Church leader did not lessen their sense of closeness and communion with him.

"He was never a distant figure; he seemed approachable," said Mrs. Dermody. "In terms of the hierarchy of the Church, it was neat to see a kindred spirit in the pope," she added.

"Ask The Pope"

Perhaps some of the closeness was strengthened by a question-and-answer period with the pope on the evening of the prayer vigil. He answered at least a dozen questions asked by the youth of Argentina through a national campaign entitled "What Would You Ask the Pope?"

All the talking and praying seemed to do both the pope and the young people good. "The pope had been so tired, because the day before he met the young people, he had visited ten cities," said Nieves Tapia. "But during the youth meeting he was so happy, and he became more relaxed."

The young people said they felt invigorated as well—and certainly not from rest. According to Mrs. Dermody, the event was a "mixture of exhaustion and excitement."

Maureen Matthews, who was sixteen when she attended the rally with the Washington group, called the World Youth Day activities "rejuvenating, especially for teenagers who have a lot of

"Here he comes!" Youth wave palms and flags to greet the pope.

"Strange brew!" The Holy Father sips *maté,* a native drink made from the dried leaves of a South American evergreen tree.

doubts." She said the exposure to so many other young believers gave her a "global vision" of Catholicism.

Chris Adams, a member of the Harrisburg (Pennsylvania) Diocese, was also impressed with the vast number of young people expressing their faith. He said it dispelled the widespread idea that young people care only about themselves, and it also showed him "the Church isn't so big. She can be very tangible if you'd like her to be."

> **"Right there, one thing was clear; we had one common faith, and that's why we were there."**

Martinez said he felt God's presence in the unity among all the participants, because "everyone treated each other like brothers and sisters."

One Big Party

To look around and see hundreds of thousands of teens and young adults praying and singing not only helped participants in their understanding of the Church, but it also showed those who watched the events on local television "a fresh, different face of the Church," said Nieves Tapia. The image before both viewers and participants was characterized not so much by speeches as by the mood of the young people themselves. In many ways they set the tone for future World Youth Days by the traditions they inaugurated.

The lack of a dress code and of sleep was certainly one of the traditions begun with the 1987 World Youth Day. The young people came to the prayer vigil in t-shirts and shorts, and they reserved their spots for the following day's Mass by camping out right there on the street, which had been blocked off for two days. Into the early morning hours, amid a few rain showers, the air was filled with the sounds of young people singing, praying, talking and dancing.

"The spirit of the crowd stood out to me; it was like a big party," said Maureen Matthews.

Martinez described being among the tens of thousands of young people as "a learning experience" and the most impressive part of the festivities. Because he spoke Spanish, he was able to talk to many of the Latin Americans throughout the night. "Right there, one thing was clear; we had one common faith, and that's why we were there," he said.

Many participants took part in what was to be a World Youth Day tradition by walking for several hours in a pilgrimage to the shrine of Our Lady of Lujan, patroness of Argentina.

"It was a long walk, but you lost sight of how hard it was. You didn't feel it when you were talking with everyone," said Martinez.

The pope had entrusted the World Youth Day participants to Our Lady of Lujan at the conclusion of the event, saying they were the hope of the Church, the evangelizers of the third millennium and witnesses of the love of Christ.

"Grant that, with the help of your grace, they may respond as you have done to the promises of Christ," he prayed.

His prayers seemed to be answered immediately, for young people from around the globe responded without hesitation and with cheers and applause to the pope's challenges.

"If this isn't Church, what is?" the youth

> "Christ draws you here; it is he who calls you."

rally crowd shouted over and over in Spanish.

The pope praised their enthusiasm, likening it to the crowd's excitement at the original celebration of Palm Sunday. But he also cautioned against excitement alone, saying, "It does not last long. It can come to an end in a matter of a day." He urged them to commit their "youthful energies to the construction of the civilization of love."

What Young People Are Really Looking For

Pope John Paul II emphasized that the crowds who gathered in both Buenos Aires and in St. Peter's Square in previous years did not simply come together for youth gatherings but because, "Christ draws you here; it is he who calls you."

"You, too, young people, will reach a full understanding of the meaning of your lives, your vocation, by looking at Christ in his death and Resurrection," he said.

Martinez had the job of providing his English-speaking group with an immediate translation of the pope's words, when he could "keep up." He said the pope continuously showed that he cared for young people and that, for him, they were a priority. He also pointed them to God—"what young people are really looking for." "The pope started a flame," he said, "now it must be kept alive."

The pope insisted that the excitement and fire the youth possessed during their time together in Buenos Aires could continue to burn only if the participants came to know Christ more fully.

In his closing words, he urged them to take up the task of understanding Christ: "Listen to [Christ's] words. Learn them deeply. Build your lives with the words and the life of Christ ever before you. Even more: learn to be Christ himself, by being identified with him in everything."

CHAPTER 3

Pilgrimage To The "End of the Earth"

Spain's Santiago trail—known for centuries as a route for religious pilgrimage—was turned over to young people from all over the world on August 16-20, 1989. Tens of thousands of teenagers and young adults jammed the ancient path not only to retrace the steps of early Christians but to receive a commission from the pope to be the world's "new apostles."

"The hour has come for reevange-lization. And you cannot be found wanting in this urgent call," Pope John Paul II told the five hundred thousand young people at World Youth Day 1989. He urged them to accept the Gospel mandate to be Christ's witnesses to the "end of the earth."

In fact, the young people were gathered in the city once known as the last major city before the end of the earth—Santiago de Compostela, in northwest Spain. They arrived by plane, boat, bus, bicycle and horse to take part in the ancient pilgrimage to the cathedral where the tomb of St. James the Apostle is said to be located.

The young people from at least eighty countries chose more up-to-date versions of the traditional pilgrims' garb. Most wore jeans and t-shirts instead of the typical pilgrim's cloak; they sported baseball caps instead of broad-brimmed hats; and they carried backpacks, tents and their national flags instead of the pilgrim's staff.

But the intention of the young pilgrims was the same as that of the thousands of pilgrims in ages before them. They followed a route taken since the ninth century to the Cathedral of Santiago de Compostela, named for St. James. The cathedral, once on a par with Rome and Jerusalem as a pilgrimage site, had been known in its heyday to draw such figures as St. Bernard of Clairvaux, St. Francis of Assisi and St. Isabella of Portugal.

In The Footsteps of the Apostles

Travel had not been quite so convenient in medieval times, and pilgrims had often faced many dangers and difficulties in their voyage. Still, they had come in droves, hoping to obtain special graces or the forgiveness of sins at the burial site of the first martyred apostle.

St. James and his brother St. John the

> They sported baseball caps instead of broad-brimmed hats; they carried backpacks and tents instead of the pilgrim's staff. But the intention of the young pilgrims was the same as that of the thousands of pilgrims in ages before them.

At the end of the traditional route of pilgrims for more than a thousand years, with staff in hand and wearing a pilgrim's short cloak on his shoulders, the pope approached the tomb of St. James and prayed, "With you, St. James, apostle and pilgrim, we want to teach the nations of Europe and the world that Christ is—today and always—the way, the truth and the life."

Evangelist were called "sons of thunder" by Jesus because of their forceful personalities. St. James was beheaded by King Herod around the year 44. According to medieval Spanish documents, his remains were taken from Jerusalem and brought to Spain, where he had preached. The tomb remained hidden for centuries and was rediscovered only during the first half of the ninth century. Although some dispute the account, the tradition has been upheld by many, making St. James the patron saint of Spain.

"At the tomb of St. James, we want to learn that our faith has historical foundations; it is not something vague and transient," Pope John Paul II had said in 1988, when he invited young people to join him at Santiago. He urged them always to remember that their faith is "built up on the stable foundation of the apostles, with Christ himself as the cornerstone."

When the pontiff arrived at Santiago, he said he felt "truly overcome by the emotion enkindled in the hearts of thousands and thousands of pilgrims" through the centuries, and he hoped the World Youth Day pilgrims would be an equally impressive sign to today's world.

The modern-day pilgrims walked for two hours to reach Monte del Gozo, a dusty mountain that would serve as a natural amphitheatre for a prayer vigil and Mass. During the hike, they talked, sang and prayed the Rosary. They were greeted by waves and cheers from residents along the route dotted with churches, abbeys and hospices.

"There was a real sense of anticipation, knowing we would all be together soon," said Maureen Kelly, from Pauling, New York. "Of course there was a cost involved too; there were no bathrooms along the way, and a lot of people got hungry or tired."

On the Way Up

Stephen Kostas, a youth delegate from Indianapolis, said the pilgrimage was one of the best parts of the World Youth Day gathering. "It was unbelievable to walk with about twenty people abreast, with everyone singing songs in his own language," he said.

A high point, literally, for eighteen-year-old Kostas was when he reached the top of a hill and could see a "caravan" of young people in front of him. "The theme of pilgrimage was discussed at length, but here was definitely a visualization of it," he said.

Once they arrived on Monte del Gozo, which means Hill of Joy, most of the young people were there to stay, reserving their spot for the next day's Mass.

> During the hike, they talked, sang and prayed the Rosary. They were greeted by waves and cheers from residents along the route.

The Holy Father told the young people that they came to Monte del Gozo with hopeful anticipation "truly to meet Jesus," who called each of them to follow him. A young woman receives Holy Communion from the pope.

"What do you seek, pilgrims?" the pope asked the young people, many of whom could only see him through their binoculars. "Each of us here must ask himself this question. But above all, since you have your life ahead of you, I invite you to decide definitely the direction of your way."

"As I saw the crowds fill up the mountain, I got the sense that this must be what it was like when crowds of people came to Galilee to hear Jesus," said Maureen Kelly, who attended the rally with other members of Youth for a United World, a branch of the Catholic lay movement called Focolare.

Stephen Kostas, who was selected as one of the young people to sit on the platform with the pope, said his memory of the crowd is a little blurry because he was "incredibly nervous and overwhelmed." From his perspective, he said the thousands of participants were "like little dots on the horizon."

During the prayer vigil, the pope gave a talk in three parts, corresponding to the three elements of the World Youth Day theme: "The Way, the Truth and the Life." Each part was introduced with a dramatic presentation by some of the Spanish youth.

Throughout his talk, the pope continued to emphasize the idea of pilgrimage. He not only addressed the young people as pilgrims, he pointed out that they were at a crossroads and urged them to move forward.

"What do you seek, pilgrims?" the pope asked the young people, many of whom could see him only through their binoculars. "Each of us here must ask himself this question. But above all, since you have your life ahead of you, I invite you to decide definitely the direction of your way," he said.

Plain Talk From The Holy Father

He told the young people that they came to Monte del Gozo with hopeful anticipation truly to "meet Jesus," who called each of them to follow him. To follow Christ, he said, was to protect human life in all its stages, to respect the call of marriage and family and to become "messengers of truth" in the world. He told them they had to bring the Gospel message to other young people like themselves, "because today, all over the world, many of them are in search of the way, the truth and the life." Pope John Paul II spoke plainly with the young people, and they did not seem to mind.

During the vigil, a youth representative told the pope, "We young people want to take up the task of proclaiming consistently that only in Jesus Christ can we find the full truth of the human person, perfect happiness and an authentic life worthy of the children of God.... We are with you! Count on us always!"

Maureen Kelly said she was willing to take up the pope's challenge because he expressed such faith in young people—a belief that they could be effective evangelists.

"When the pope spoke to us it was as if he was talking to each one of us personally," she said. "He was so honest. He spoke as authentically as possible and challenged us." She said she was filled with a willingness to stand up for her beliefs, even if it would mean persecution, because she knew for the first time that she was not alone in her faith. "I used to ask, 'God, am I the only young practicing Catholic?'" But after nearly a week in Santiago with half a million other young believers, she said she realized she was far from alone.

Stephen Kostas agreed. He said his faith increased more from seeing people his own age express their faith than from hearing the pope's message. He said he was not completely surprised to see crowds of young people praying, singing, attending Mass and lining up for confession. "It didn't strike me as odd in that setting, but it would strike me as odd in Bloomington, Indiana," he added.

Camping Out

The young people who filled Santiago did not pray all the time. They danced in the streets and talked and sang late into the night. Like a festival, the city was alive with concerts, rallies and crowds everywhere.

Tens of thousands of young people stayed in a tent city set up by the Spanish army. The "city" was without normal conveniences young people might want. Showers were limited, as were beauty rest and time for hair-styling; food was scooped onto trays, military style.

"People think young people are frivolous and superficial, but here we were not. We were there for a different thing—for something grander," said Maureen Kelly.

Not only did the young people have to wait in line for rest rooms and water, many had to communicate with their hands, since they spoke different languages.

"We used gestures and spoke slowly. You had to be patient," said Jonathan Broussard, a youth delegate from Orange, Texas.

He said he felt as if he could understand people, even though they spoke different languages, simply because they shared the same faith and encountered many of the same difficulties in their daily lives.

Chris Sherman, another youth delegate from Texas, agreed. He described the experience of being with the other young people from around the world as a "global village."

Opposite page: To the group of people receiving the symbolic staffs, the pope said, "As you go back to your churches and to your work, take with you this pilgrim's staff in order to walk always toward Christ, the way, the truth and the life for the whole world. May the staff you carry in your hands remind you that you are the missionary Church and, above all, that you must lean on Christ in order to proclaim his message of salvation for every person, every family, every people."

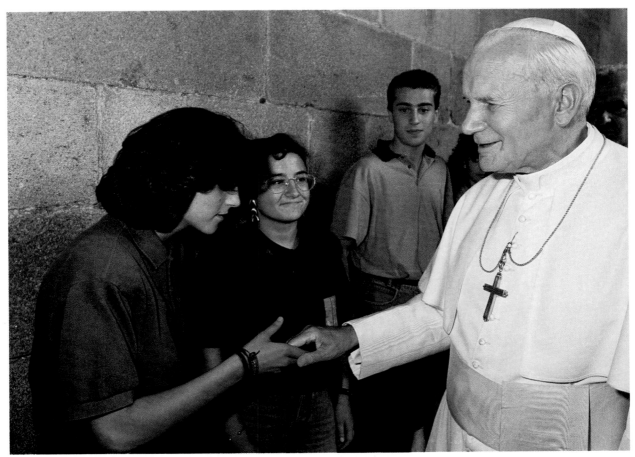

"Put 'er there!" The Holy Father goes out to the young people gathered at Santiago de Compostela and, believing in their ability to be effective evangelists, tells them that to follow Christ, they must become **"messengers of the truth"** in the world.

An Immediate Sense Of Mission

In the days before the pope arrived in Santiago, the young people spent time getting to know each other and getting to know more about their faith through various talks given in local churches by bishops and cardinals from around the world.

And even though they had only two days with the pope, they seemed to get to know him, too, as shown by their constant shouts of "Viva el papa!"

"He's extremely young looking, and he has an energy about him," said Kostas, one of the few who saw the pontiff up close.

Maureen Kelly, who saw the pope from a distance, said she "really had a sense he loves young people in the Church."

Perhaps they felt so close to the Roman Catholic leader since he joined them in part of their pilgrimage to the Cathedral of Santiago de Compostela. With a staff in hand and wearing a pilgrim's short cloak on his shoulders, the pope approached the tomb of St. James and prayed, "With you, St. James, apostle and pilgrim, we want to

> **During the closing Mass, when he said, "Do not be afraid to be saints," the crowd burst into applause.**

teach the nations of Europe and the world that Christ is—today and always—the way, the truth and the life."

He told the young people they were called to be apostles just like St. James, a man who was brash and determined and also willing to follow Christ to his own death.

The pope never stopped emphasizing that all young people could follow Christ with the same zeal. During the closing Mass, when he said, "Do not be afraid to be saints," the crowd burst into applause.

His words gave the young people an immediate sense of mission.

"Teenagers get tired of hearing they are the future of the Church," said Sherman, who said the pope's message was that they could be active members of the Church now, not years down the road.

"I walked away realizing my part in the Church and my responsibility to the Church," said Maureen Kelly.

She said the World Youth Day event "sealed something" in her soul, so that "no matter how difficult things may be, I know there's a bigger reality."

Stephen Kostas could not help but walk away with a sense of mission, particularly since he was one of ten young people from different continents selected to receive a pilgrim's staff from the pope at the close of the World Youth Day celebration.

"I was, to say the least, overwhelmed by the role and very humbled," he said.

Speaking in German, the pope asked him if he were German. Although Kostas barely knew German, he realized what the pope was saying and told him No, he was American. "That broke the ice. The pope chuckled and we shook hands," said

Kostas. "When he handed me the staff, he said he wanted me to go out and fulfill God's words. That was too much for me as an eighteen-year-old!"

To the group of people receiving the symbolic staffs, the pope said, "As you go back to your churches and to your work, take with you this pilgrim's staff in order to walk always toward Christ, the way, the truth and the life for the whole world. May the staff you carry in your hands remind you that you are the missionary Church and, above all, that you must lean on Christ in order to proclaim his message of salvation for every person, every family, every people."

This is no time for a siesta! The pope urges the half-million young people gathered for World Youth Day '89 to accept the Gospel mandate to be Christ's witnesses to the "end of the earth." "The hour has come for re-evangelization. And you cannot be found wanting in this urgent call."

CHAPTER 4

"The Russians Are Coming!"

For five days in mid-August of 1991, the small industrial center of Czestochowa in southern Poland was taken by storm by thousands of singing and praying young people from all around the world. Although many of them came by plane, bus or train, a large number of them walked from bordering countries.

Tens of thousands of young people walking from the Soviet Union arrived late after having been detained at their own border. When they were seen marching triumphantly over the horizon, an onlooker shouted "The Russians are coming! The Russians are coming!"

The huge group had been identified by their then-traditional flag with a hammer and sickle. "You could hear them getting louder and happier" as they approached, said youth delegate Tina Purcell from Milford, Delaware. It was the first time the Soviet government had allowed its citizens to attend a religious youth rally, and at least seventy thousand young people took advantage of the opportunity. It was a turning point in history. One and a half million teenagers and young adults from around the world celebrated their faith with the pope in his native land.

It was the first time a World Youth Day had been held in a former Communist country. The event took place only two years after the end of the Cold War, and it ended three days before an attempted coup in the former Soviet Union would ultimately lead to the fall of Communism there.

"The young people from Russia didn't have

A young women kneels in prayer. In his parting challenge to the crowd of young people the pope told them, "Be demanding of the world around you; be demanding first of all with yourselves. Be children of God; take pride in it!... Christ is calling you to do great things. Do not disappoint him. You would be disappointing yourselves."

anything; they didn't have any food," said Virginia Miksch, from Texas, who was sixteen when she

The Holy Father, Pope John Paul II, and one and a half million of his closest friends—the teenagers and young adults from around the world, celebrating their common faith in his native Poland.

attended the rally. "We shared what we had with them, because here we had bottles of Evian in our backpacks."

The World Turned Upside-down

Those who had walked for days to attend the celebration might not have had many belongings, but they were not without stories of faith.

"They were so joyful and glad they could come," said Allison Boyle of Gaithersburg, Maryland. She said the young people from former Communist countries spoke of how their "faith had triumphed," and how their "faith was the only thing they had to hold onto."

The historical significance of recent events could not help but be felt by everyone during the World Youth Day. "Huge things had recently happened in the world," said Bryan Hersey, a delegate from St. Paul, Minnesota. "Just two years before, Poland was fairly closed off and here we were all meeting there just as young people on equal footing. It gave me a real sense that countries are transient but the Church is a little more established."

But even the established Catholic Church had experienced her struggles. It was not until 1989, the year the Berlin Wall fell and the Cold War ended, that the Polish parliament restored legal status to the Church for the first time since 1944. With the new laws, Catholics could worship freely, recover Church property confiscated by the government, build churches and teach religion.

During the 1970s, the Polish bishops, including the bishop who became Pope John Paul II, had made a solemn act of entrusting the Church and the world to the Madonna at the shrine of Our Lady of Czestochowa, where the young people gathered in mid-August.

The shrine, Poland's most important

Pope John Paul II gives a fatherly kiss to a World Youth Day delegate in Poland.

pilgrimage site, sits atop a hill of white rock named Jasna Gora, meaning "bright mountain." It is visited each year by between two and three million people.

"The Black Madonna"

According to tradition, St. Luke the Evangelist painted the image of Mary on a wooden panel from the Holy Family's house in Nazareth. The icon, moved to Czestochowa in the fourteenth century, was slashed with a knife by a group of bandits in 1430. The resulting scars give the painting one of its names, the Madonna of the Wounded Face. The darkness of the image of Mary also led it to be called the Black Madonna.

The site of the chapel and monastery, run by the order of St. Paul the Hermit, has been the scene of many battles over the past six centuries. After withstanding a forty-day siege by Swedish troops in 1655, the icon in the ancient shrine received yet another title—Queen of Poland.

> It was the first time the Soviet government had allowed its citizens to attend a religious youth rally, and at least seventy thousand young people took advantage of the opportunity.

"...At the threshold of a new spiritual season for mankind, I pray that young people from East and West will walk together along the path of freedom, working to overcome all conflicts between races and peoples, so as to build a world of authentic brotherhood and carry the liberating message of the Gospel everywhere."

—Pope John Paul II

During World Youth Day 1991, the pilgrimage site was a far cry from a battleground, although young soldiers from Poland, France, Italy, Hungary, Germany, Spain, Austria and the then-Czechoslovakia assembled there. They were just a portion of the crowd from eighty different countries whom the pope addressed in twenty-three different languages.

"It was a worldwide Church experience," said youth delegate Kristina Kerscher, a graduate student at the University of Dayton in Ohio. "I realized the Church was so big," said Brian Hersey, a senior at St. John Vianney Seminary in St. Paul, Minnesota.

The thousands of young people stayed in youth hostels and dorms. They camped in school classrooms and auditoriums and under the stars in what was described by many as a summer camp. Their singing, praying, talking and dancing lasted well into the night. Throughout the day, sound-system speakers on the main road continuously broadcast music and prayers.

Holy Father Gets a "Standing O"

To attend the August 14 prayer vigil, the young people had to squeeze through the narrow mile-and-a-half road leading to the shrine, holding hands in order to stay together.

That night they greeted the pope with a twenty-minute chanting, singing and standing ovation. Many could not see him at all; others said he looked about an inch tall, and some worked their way through the crowd on top of friends' shoulders to get a glimpse of him.

As part of a World Youth Day tradition, most of the young people reserved their spot for the next day's Mass by staying there overnight with a limited supply of rest rooms, food and sleep.

During the Mass, Pope John Paul II encouraged the young people to "offer the world a public demonstration" of belonging to Christ and the Church in front of their peers from every part of the globe.

"After a long period of practically impassable borders, the Church in Europe can breathe freely now with both her lungs," he said. "Your presence, my dear young people of Eastern Europe, takes on particular significance. The universal Church needs the precious treasure of your Christian witness."

Pope John Paul II told the young people from former Communist countries that their time had finally come. He assured them that the Church had not forgotten about them during their time of suffering and that she was counting on them now to spread the good news.

A New Challenge Ahead

He did not paint a picture of an Eastern Europe in which all was going well simply because the Iron Curtain had fallen. In fact, the pope told the participants in the rally that the collapse of Communist ideology had "left the feeling of a great vacuum in many of your companions, the impression of having been deceived and a depressing anguish in the face of what is to come."

The pope acknowledged that many people even in Western Europe had "lost their motivation for living," as proven by the problem of drug addiction.

In light of the world's suffering and confusion, he commissioned the young people to be "messengers of the good news of salvation" so that others would "discover the meaning of life by encountering Jesus Christ."

Calling Jasna Gora the upper room of a "new Pentecost," the pope told the young people to receive the Holy Spirit and to be renewed

> That night they greeted the pope with a twenty-minute chanting, singing and standing ovation.

in their commission to build a new world. "Let this fire blaze in your heart. Take it to every part of the globe. May it never be extinguished by anything."

As the pope gave his message in several languages, the young people, clad in shorts and T-shirts, listened to instant translations through headsets or hand-held radios.

Joel Beauvais had the only radio for his group of about thirty people from Meriden, Connecticut. He held it to his ear and simultaneously told the group what the pope was saying. "What an experience to be saying the pope's words as his amplifier," he said.

One member of his group, Nathan Havill, said the pope's message of courage and hope impressed him. "It showed us there is a place for young people in the Church."

"He Wanted to Talk to Us"

Kristina Kerscher, who was selected to read one of the readings during the prayer vigil, was not convinced at first that she would be awed by the pontiff. "Like most Americans my age, I didn't think it would be such a big deal to be near the pope," she said. "But when he came on the altar and was ten feet away from me, I had a real experience of holiness."

The young woman said she cried but insisted it was not "out of an emotional frenzy." When she finished reading, the pope smiled at her and blessed her. "That expression defied all logic," she said. "It said something about God's love that goes beyond all human understanding."

For many young people, the small actions of the pope were just as significant as his speeches. Some recalled how the pontiff hugged one young woman from Sudan who spoke during the August 15 Mass.

In Sudanese, the young woman told the World Youth Day participants about the terrible oppression in her country, and she cried out for

Hup, Two, Three, Four! Bearing the standard of Christ crucified, young people on the march to the Shrine of Our Lady of Czestochowa—Poland's most important pilgrimage site atop a hill of white rock named Jasna Gora, meaning "bright mountain."

help from people of other nations. When she finished speaking, she ran to greet the pope but was stopped by security guards. The pope not only shook his head to stop the guards; he also got up from his chair and hugged her.

"I had heard a lot about his love for young people, but this put a stamp on it," said Brian Hersey.

Carol Collins, who attended the rally with a group of people from *You!* magazine, said that that action stands out to her more than anything else the pope did. "It's what I'll remember about how he wanted to talk to us," she said.

You Are Not Alone!

Although the teens and young adults were enamored of the pope's compassion and sense of humor, they were equally awed by the number of people their age expressing a love for God and the Catholic faith.

"It was totally packed. It blew my mind," said Allison Boyle, who attended the rally with a group of students from schools run by Opus Dei.

Many said they realized for the first time that they were not alone in their beliefs. "It let us know there are other people out there just like us, with the same hopes and fears, even if they speak different languages," said Brian Hersey.

Kimberly Hunter, who came with the group from Connecticut, said that "the most amazing experience was the fact that there were so many people my age absolutely in love with their faith." She said the impact of the event changed her, so much so that she planned to enter the religious life to be a Franciscan sister. And again, she did not feel alone. She said she had heard that "one thousand young people have gone into some type of religious life after that World Youth Day."

So the lessons from Czestochowa have continued to sink in long after the young people caught up on their missing sleep.

They Keep in Touch

Carol Collins said the significance of the event did not "click" until a few months after she came home. "People asked me, 'What did you do this summer?' and I said, 'Well, I went to Poland. Well, I saw the pope.' When I was there, I was so caught up with meeting new people that I didn't realize how special it was."

But meeting new people and getting pictures taken with flags from across the world was not an event to be downplayed. Today, many of the participants continue to keep in touch with the people they met. They write letters and pray for the friends they now have in war-torn countries.

"I definitely came back not so much in my own world," said Allison Boyle.

> "Be demanding of the world around you; be demanding first of all with yourselves. Be children of God; take pride in it!..."

Joel Beauvais said it was not until he came home and started talking about the experience with his friends that he realized its impact. "I guess we were a little like the apostles, because we never got what was going on while it was happening."

Virginia Miksch was also quick to say that the event changed her. "I've done a lot of things I wouldn't have done before. Now I take more of a stand on things."

Clearly that was one of the pope's intentions. In his parting challenge to the crowd of young people, he said, "Be demanding of the world around you; be demanding first of all with yourselves. Be children of God; take pride in it! ... Christ is calling you to do great things. Do not disappoint him. You would be disappointing yourselves."

A few days later, while crews were cleaning the hillside of Jasna Gora, the pope told a general audience at the Vatican that the 1991 World Youth Day celebration "served as a powerful reminder" to young people "of the fundamental role which they must play in the new evangelization of humanity."

"At the shrine of Jasna Gora, with its ancient image of the Black Madonna, those present were able to experience together a turning point of history and to recover, after the sufferings of our century and the collapse of ideologies, the Christian roots of Europe. At the threshold of a new spiritual season for mankind, I pray that young people from East and West will walk together along the path of freedom, working to overcome all conflicts between races and peoples, so as to build a world of authentic brotherhood and carry the liberating message of the Gospel everywhere."

"Denver, Here We Come!"

"Don't even think twice about (not going) because it's an experience that will mark your life forever," Chris Hickman of Montreal said as he and youths around the world prepared for World Youth Day '93 in Denver.

"When you see . . . young people from all around the world who are believing in this religion," said Hickman, "it really solidifies it for you, and it becomes real and makes you realize that it's OK to be a teenager and be Catholic at the same time."

His enthusiasm typified the feelings of youths as they got ready financially, spiritually and physically for the youth events with Pope John Paul II in the "Mile High City."

For the pope, youths and Denver were never far from his thoughts since April 1992 when he announced the site for World Youth Day '93. "Denver, Colorado, in the beautiful Rockies" was on his lips whenever he met young people during the months leading up to the international event.

And Denver was in the hearts and on the minds of youths and their parents, youth ministers, parishes and dioceses as they figured out just how they were going to get there.

One Polish youth was so eager to attend World Youth Day she arrived in Denver two months early.

Malgorzata Faber, 17, from Zielona Gora, Poland, had been to World Youth Day in 1991 in Czestochowa, and she was determined to reach the Colorado gathering. She worked two jobs, as a waitress and a housekeeper, to pay for her plane ticket.

She arrived in Denver with no place to stay — the friends who were going to put her up had moved away — but a good Samaritan she met on her flight helped her find quarters through a local parish.

She admitted to being "a little brave," but said "I had power from above. I have faith in God."

For most dioceses generating interest and spreading the word was the first step. According to one World Youth Day organizer, before some bishops could "sell" the event to the youths of their dioceses, young people were telling them they wanted to go.

In at least one diocese getting the word out involved challenges of distance.

Diarmuid O'Donovan in White Horse, in Canada's Yukon Territory, had an awesome job — he had to reach young people spread across 289,000 square miles. Notices went out to even the tiniest communities. Once that was done, the next phase was raising the money for the trip.

As elsewhere, fund raising in the Yukon had a certain local flavor. Where else could nuggets of gold from the Klondike have been raffled off? That and other efforts brought in $53,000 and put 76 youths on a plane for Denver.

When they boarded they wore matching jackets and hats bearing the World Youth Day logo. Around their necks on a leather lace hung crosses made from Yukon willow, a symbol of love

On Palm Sunday, 1992, a delegation from the United States accepts the World Youth Day pilgrim cross at a ceremony in St. Peter's Square.

— and a labor of love for O'Donovan's wife, Kathy.

The efforts of the O'Donovans and the youths in the Yukon were repeated across Canada as well as across the United States and the other countries that sent young people to Denver to be with the pope and with each other. By the time World Youth Day was under way, 71 countries — from Angola to Zimbabwe — were represented by tens of thousands of youths.

Their ideas for fund raising seemed limited only by the imagination. There were: flea markets, Christmas tree and wreath sales, a golf tournament, baby sitting, dog walking, house painting and cleaning, pancake breakfasts, Easter flower and palm cross sales, a chili feed and bingo party, Sunday morning breakfasts, turkey raffles, sales of Christmas and Easter cards, and pop can and bottle drives.

Youths offered to iron clothes, clean out attics and rake leaves. They square-danced the

> **By the time World Youth Day was under way, seventy-one countries–from Angola to Zimbabwe–were represented by tens of thousands of young people.**

night away. They had yard sales and sponsor-a-teen programs. One group thought up the "family photo opportunity," in which a local photo studio took family portraits and donated the $6 fee to youths. There were poster and essay contests and in at least one place a lip-sync contest.

Fund raising in the St. Cloud Diocese in Minnesota had such a strong emphasis on food that Benedictine Sister Nancy Bauer, in a tongue-in-cheek column in the St. Cloud Visitor, the diocesan newspaper, accused the youth of being involved in a "conspiracy ... to make the rest of us get fat."

Passing a marshmallow is one of "101 Things to do on the Bus" practiced by two youths of the Gary, Indiana diocese in preparation for their long ride to Denver.

A "HOG Wash" helped raise money for a youth group from St. Clare's parish in North Lake, Wisconsin. Young people there took advantage of the ninetieth anniversary of the local Harley-Davidson Company to raise money for their trip to Denver. They scrubbed as many Harleys—affectionately called "HOGs," for the Harley Owners' Group—as they could at $10 apiece.

"Cow Kissing" and Letterman's Cap

When youth groups at St. Philip Neri and Holy Cross parishes in the Indianapolis Archdiocese were "in a crunch" for more money, youth ministry volunteer Paul Okerson wrote to some celebrities to donate something to an auction.

The results? Among the items he received were an NBC "Late Night With David Letterman" baseball cap and sweatshirt from the comedian himself; a sweatshirt signed by talk show host Oprah Winfrey; a photo and CD from singer Amy Grant; a baseball cap and key chain from University of Notre Dame football coach Lou Holtz; and autographed racing cards from Indianapolis 500 racing favorites Mario, Michael and Jeff Andretti.

In Fargo, N.D., they had a "carol-gram." People made a free-will offering to send Catholic Youth Organization carolers to a specific house.

In New Orleans, youths made versions of the popular local sandwich — the "po-boy." For youths in Rene Villeger's rural community of Hythe, Alberta, it meant auctioning off a steer. Eighty-year-old Father Pierre Pouellet in Fort Nelson, British Columbia, started hooking a rug that eventually sold at a raffle for $1,300.

A "HOG Wash" brought in money in Milwaukee. Youths at one parish took advantage of the 90th anniversary of the local Harley-Davidson Co. to raise money for WYD. They scrubbed as many Harleys — affectionately called "HOGs" for the Harley Owners' Group — as they could at $10 apiece.

In the Diocese of Rochester, N.Y., Father David Gramkee at St. Patrick's Church and two parishioners solicited pledges for promising to kiss a cow.

The youth group at St. Anthony Parish in Red Bank, N.J., even benefited from a "nor'easter" which ripped through the shore area during December '92. "The storm helped us out," Rainville said. "The kids cleaned and raked people's yards."

Car washes were big. But not just in the United States. About 12,000 Italian youths headed to Denver could swap stories with their peers about shriveled fingers and soaked jeans. Car washes were the most common group fund-raising effort for them.

Financial help for Central and East European youth came in the form of scholarships made possible by a national U.S. collection for the Catholic Church in that part of the world.

The youths came from the Czech Republic, Slovakia, Hungary, Poland, Romania, Bulgaria, Croatia, Slovenia, Albania, Lithuania, Latvia, Estonia, Russia, Siberia, Bielarus, Kazakhstan and Ukraine. The money helped offset travel and lodging expenses to allow the young people, who lived their childhood under the religious suppression of communist rule, to join their Western peers in an open celebration of their Catholic faith.

"Our nation and our church have experienced a difficult and heavy journey," said Viktor Makovskii, a seminarian in the Ukrainian Diocese of Zytomir. "And while there is a great economic crisis before us, there is yet an even bigger crisis confronting the spirit of our young, caused by the deception of communist ideology. Our principal task, that of tomorrow's priests, will be to lead our young through this crisis."

In addition to the group traveling on scholarships, another 20 Russian youths made it to World Youth Day, thanks to U.S. dioceses that volunteered to host them. In late July the Russians arrived in Washington, D.C., for a week of orientation and sightseeing. Then, before reaching Denver, it was on to their host dioceses to live with a local family and learn about the local culture, emphasizing "the faith life of youth in America."

Soul Searching

Money and how to raise it made up only part of the preparations for World Youth Day '93.

On the spiritual side, youth day organizers wanted to instill a spirit of pilgrimage in World Youth Day.

The U.S. bishops declared a year of preparation which included resource manuals being sent to diocesan contacts and parishes, Catholic colleges, campus ministry groups and Catholic high schools. Activities and prayers focused on the theme from John 10:10: "I came so that they might have life and have it more abundantly."

Archbishop William H. Keeler of Baltimore, who as president of the U.S. bishops' conference was chairman of its Ad Hoc Committee for World Youth Day, called the event a "1990s pilgrimage with sneakers replacing sandals and modern transportation replacing camel and horse."

Denver and the rest of the United States have no grand pilgrimage tradition like Europe and Latin America. So, to foster the pilgrimage concept, World Youth Day organizers picked several hub cities a day's travel or more outside of Denver as

Opposite page: "Take me to your leader!" Scanning the earth for signs of intelligent spiritual life, a "UFB" (unidentified blimp) happens across young people in Austin, Texas, forming a human cross to kick off their preparations for World Youth Day.

meeting places so that young people in buses and cars could form caravans from there to Denver.

Salt Lake City, Utah, was one of the hubs. There organizers brought together about 3,000 pilgrims with singing, praying and Scripture. A prayer service — with prayers recited in several languages — held on a soccer field at the state fair grounds launched the caravans from there.

Other hubs included Albuquerque, New Mexico, San Antonio, Texas, Boise, Idaho, Rapid City, South Dakota, Wichita and Salina, Kansas, Omaha, Nebraska, Indianapolis, Indiana and Memphis, Tennesee.

To rally people to join the pilgrimage of World Youth Day a special youth cross was carried to about 42 dioceses around the United States. First given by the pope to youth in 1984, the cross has been handed on from one delegation of young people to another for each of the international gatherings.

When youths in the Byzantine Diocese of Parma, Ohio, received the cross, they had three days of special events, including a retreat, an all-night vigil, a bonfire and a one-mile procession.

"The cross," Bishop Andrew Pataki told them, "is a sign of God's love, mercy and forgiveness." He told them to be witnesses to Christ in every aspect of their lives.

In the Boston Archdiocese, Cardinal Bernard F. Law led a Pilgrimage Walk. Also young people came together twice a month to pray and prepare for the Denver gathering.

Beginning in November, Father Paul Juniet, a Franciscan priest at Sacred Heart Parish in Farmington, New Mexico, walked each day leading up to World Youth Day. His

> **Pilgrims were encouraged to pray daily, focus on a spiritual goal and be open to whatever trials and tribulations came their way.**

After the World Youth Day cross made it back to the States, it started "making the rounds." Young people in Indianapolis carry the cross in preparation for the big event in Denver.

goal was 1,000 miles. He collected pledges but also got into great physical shape for the youth day's 15-mile pilgrimage from downtown Denver to Cherry Creek State Park, site of the closing Mass with the pope.

Father Juniet called the international gathering an occasion to "value our youth and value our faith.... A witness...to the goodness of youth" and their spirituality.

Be Prepared for Anything

To give youths at St. Anne in Le Sueur, Minnesota, the clear picture of the pilgrimage, organizers wanted them to understand that they might have to endure some inconvenience, hardship and a lot of waiting. Youth director Terry Keenan purposely kept her youths waiting by arriving late for meetings.

She also encouraged the pilgrims to pray daily, focus on a spiritual goal and be open to whatever trials and tribulations came their way.

For another group of Minnesotans, the pilgrimage involved heavier-duty physical training — bicycling wherever they went before leaving the state on bikes Aug. 1 to start their 1,000-mile trek to Denver. The group of about 20 riders, who ranged in age from 14 to 53, were followed by a support vehicle.

The bike trip alone lent itself "to the building of a community," said trip coordinator Carolyn Held. And about World Youth Day she added, "It's exciting to see so many young people in touch with their faith."

Many parishes had commissioning services to send off their groups of youths. Bishop Sean P. O'Malley of the Diocese of Fall River commissioned about 150 pilgrims for Denver at the close of an afternoon of picnicking and sports for youth and youth ministers in the diocese. New Orleans Archbishop Francis B. Schulte celebrated a commissioning Mass.

Young people in rural areas of the Archdiocese of Omaha, Neb., took part in "youthquakes" — rallies that included prayer, reflection, games, dancing and dinner.

Youths in one Omaha parish donned necklaces made of cockleshells, which are symbolic of pilgrimage.

Teens and young adults also met at four different sites to walk to Omaha's St. Cecilia Cathedral for Mass and fellowship.

In the Diocese of Ogdensburg, New York, about 75 youths and their chaperons spent a weekend getting to know one another, praying together and discussing being a member of a global church.

A youth rally in the Archdiocese of Atlanta sent contingents of local pilgrims on their way.

Nearly 300 youths from the Archdiocese of Washington received crosses to wear in a blessing ceremony conducted by Cardinal James A. Hickey of Washington.

Two Americas...But One Faith

Denver's Hispanic connection gave a special focus to World Youth Day. The Denver Archdiocese is one of several that have started outreach to Hispanic young people. The international youth gathering drew from the large Hispanic community in the Western United States and thousands more made the trip from Mexico and Central America.

It was an occasion for uniting youth from "the two Americas, North and South," with U.S. Hispanics as the link, according to Cardinal Eduardo F. Pironio, president of the Pontifical Council for the Laity, which sponsors World Youth Day.

For several months leading up to the event,

"C'mon guys!" Michael Hrdlicka of Fargo, North Dakota, shows the goal of a fundraiser for World Youth Day.

At Boston College High School in Boston, young people applaud at a Mass marking the pilgrimage year for World Youth Day. In addition, young people came together twice a month to pray and prepare for the Denver gathering.

Mexican-born singer Cuco Chavez traveled across the country giving concerts with the message that youths needed to prepare spiritually for the international gathering.

"I wanted to make people aware that this (was) not a vacation," he said. His concerts included dancing, singing and catechetical sessions.

At one performance for 2,000 youths in Los Angeles, he and his band gave them a variety of mariachi rhythms, Latin American salsa and merengue, plus encouragement to pray, fast, read Scripture and attend Mass, in order to prepare.

A Rocky Mountain Welcome

In the Mile High City itself, World Youth Day organizers got to work almost as soon as the pope announced it as the site for 1993.

Denver as a city was excited. Banner headlines in one of the local dailies proclaimed the event an "economy boon," noting about $145 million would be pumped into the city. Some of the city's merchants banded together to put on a public service campaign to heighten the awareness of the diversity of cultures among the pilgrims. A special exhibit of Vatican and Italian art treasurers opened in one of the museums.

Colorado farmers donated part of their wheat crop for Communion wafers for the many Masses. The effort, which the farmers dubbed "The Great Harvest," followed meetings of citizens from rural communities in eastern Colorado on how they could participate. Dorothy Kopetski from Wiggins, Colo., said the farmers were proud to know their wheat would be "offered to God and blessed by the pope."

World Youth Day organizers had to work with local law enforcement to figure out security for the event. Denver police held neighborhood meetings with residents in areas most affected by the influx of young people.

Organizers took care of logistics. They lined up thousands of volunteers, young and old, "to do everything from setting up chairs, cleaning up sites, to the ultimate of being an usher at the papal welcome or any event (with) the pope," said coordinator of volunteers Karen Harder.

Their work also included preparing roads and trails to lead into Cherry Creek State Park, the site for the final Mass with the pope. Trails had to be widened and the roads hardened at the park. One of

the first three people to volunteer was Evelyn Thiele, a member of Denver's Church of the Risen Christ Parish. Working in the media office where she helped reporters, she said, "It's the biggest event I've ever been involved in…the most exciting thing…. I wouldn't have missed it for the world!"

Lining up housing was another major task. Sites ranged from private homes to area college dorms to gymnasiums at local Catholic and public schools.

One of the more noteworthy arrangements involved the nuns at the Little Sisters of the Poor Home for the Aged. Some 80 teens who were volunteers at the order's home in the Bronx, N.Y.,

arranged to sleep in the back yard of the order's nursing home in Denver.

Mother Gonzague said the Denver residents were "overjoyed" at the New Yorkers' coming and wanted to do as much as they could for them. Some offered to give up their rooms to the youths, others made snacks and souvenirs for them. One resident even sent $100 to sponsor a youth. On their side, the youths offered a picnic and concert for the nursing home residents.

Their sharing showed the spirit of the pilgrimage: Young and old, all part of the Body of Christ, making World Youth Day in Denver an event to remember.

CHAPTER 6

"We Can Change the World"

Optimism was running high at Regis University as delegates from countries ranging from Albania to Zambia waved flags and introduced themselves at the International Youth Forum. When they gave their reasons for attending, more than one of the delegates said, "I believe we can change the face of the world."

These delegates, chosen to represent their countries' episcopal conferences or other Catholic organizations, arrived in Denver before other World Youth Day participants to attend the fourth International Youth Forum, from August 8 to 11, sponsored by the Pontifical Council for the Laity.

Dressed in native costumes—Indian saris, brightly colored African robes, Scottish kilts—as well as in the universal dress code of shorts and t-shirts, the young people gathered for what looked like a United Nations in miniature. The 270 delegates from nearly one hundred countries came to the red brick campus under bright blue skies prepared to work. They carried small clear plastic briefcases filled with papers and notebooks, and they wore headsets to hear simultaneous translations of speakers in English, French, Spanish or Italian. Many of the youth also carried language dictionaries to assist them in conversations.

They met from morning to late afternoon in general sessions and workshops to discuss social issues, challenges faced by today's Catholic youth and ways to evangelize other young people. Youth from the warring countries of Bosnia-Herzegovina, Croatia, Serbia, Slovenia and Montenegro sat together taking notes. In between sessions, groups of delegates posed in front of cameras and video recorders.

When Archbishop J. Francis Stafford of Denver welcomed the delegates to the Rocky Mountains, he urged them to contemplate issues of faith while they looked at the surrounding mountains and streams. He reminded them that Pope John Paul II, when he was their age, had often reflected on his faith and the problems of the world when he looked at nature. The archbishop also told the young people that the responsibilities ahead of them were not easy. "You are required to work very hard…with the issues facing the Church and the evangelization of cultures," he said.

We're on a Mission From God

Cardinal Eduardo Pironio, president of the Pontifical Council for the Laity and overseer of the planning for every World Youth Day since 1985, gave the keynote address at the forum's opening ceremony. Speaking on the theme "Born to New Life in Christ Jesus," the cardinal, a native of Argentina, described the youth forum as an important event— "not simply an exchange of information, ideas or of studies," but a meeting for "profound renovation, conversion and hope open to all the world."

Opposite page: "Young people need to see the practical relevance of their efforts to meet the real needs of the people, especially the poor and neglected," the pope said in his homily during a special Mass at Denver's Cathedral of the Immaculate Conception for International Youth Forum delegates.

Cardinal Pironio told the delegates that the mission of Christ was their mission, and he urged them to combat the world "marked by violence, hatred and death" by committing themselves to have the "courage to be saints." He said that young people need to be knowledgeable about their faith, strong, united and full of missionary spirit. "The Holy Spirit is stirring new generations of young people who are happy, profound and committed. This is the advent of new times," he said.

He also asked the delegates to think about the suffering caused by war, extreme hunger, injustice and oppression in many countries of the world. "There are many witnesses here today from those countries. How does that move us? Do we feel only curiosity and superficial compassion or do we experience true sorrow, active participation in that suffering and a commitment to alleviate it?" The delegates were given a glimpse of the struggles young Catholics face around the world when many of the youth spoke of the troubles in their homelands and pleaded for prayers. One of the first such testimonies was from Mario Santro, a delegate from Zagreb, Bosnia-Herzegovina, who said it was not easy to speak about his life. Young Catholics in his country had once been able to organize themselves, he said, "to carry out our mission," which was the "best way to keep our ideas, dreams and goals." But he said that the war in that region has prevented young people from continuing their work. "[We] are trying to understand why there is suffering. We wait out the pain and suffering, holding onto the [biblical] words, 'Be not afraid, my little flock.'"

Pressure!

Elena Chaka, a twenty-three-year-old from Khartoum, Sudan, told the group that the Sudanese

Pope John Paul II prays during the offertory at a Mass for delegates of the International Youth Forum while a delegate from India places a fragrant bouquet before the altar.

government has closed Christian centers and schools and "forces small children to become Muslim by giving them food and clothing.... We [Christians] will not stop our activity just because of Islamic pressures," she said. "We cannot be disgraced forever. We must speak out. The youth in Sudan suffer, and our government speaks about peace, but not seriously.... Youth over the world, pray for Sudan," she said in a soft voice.

Many of the delegates said that such witnesses opened their eyes. "The testimonies are a chance to listen, to discover the context in which these people live and grow in their faith," said Anna Przybysz from Warsaw, Poland.

Irene Szumlakowski, a delegate from Spain, described the struggles of youth in other countries as "challenges that must be faced. Young people are desperate. We cannot face problems of drugs, violence, unemployment, justice, wars in different places.... Although each country has its own particular problems, these are the problems of the world and our problems."

Another delegate, Christine Kayes from Auckland, New Zealand, did not speak of religious persecution or war but instead stressed religious indif-

> **Dressed in native costumes—Indian saris, brightly colored African robes, Scottish kilts—as well as in the universal dress code of shorts and t-shirts, the young people gathered for what looked like a United Nations in miniature.**

"Nice to see you too!" Cardinal Eduardo Pironio, President of the Pontifical Council for the Laity, leads a group of delegates across the Regis University campus for the opening of the fourth International Youth Forum.

Two hundred and seventy delegates from nearly one hundred countries converged on Denver to attend the fourth International Youth Forum. Delegates, chosen to represent their countries' episcopal conferences or other Catholic organizations, met to discuss social issues, challenges faced by today's Catholic youth, and ways to evangelize other young people.

ference, which she called an equally serious problem. "In New Zealand, life is easy," she said. "We are physically comfortable but in a spiritual desert."

She was far from alone. During breaks between sessions, many of the delegates spoke about being in the minority as believers. Roseline Urrio, a seventeen-year-old from Tanzania, described the youth in her country as "not spiritually well off. They don't like to go to church or to pray. It's a worldwide problem, I think."

Adrienne Luckey, eighteen, from Belleville, Illinois, agreed. "Very similar problems face youth all over the world. They seem to figure no place for God."

These youth were not full of gloom and despair, but instead they believed they could make a positive impact on other youth through their own example of faith, which was strengthened during the forum gathering. The delegates said their faith was given a boost not so much from the general sessions and workshops as from talking with people from other countries and sharing stories of faith over meals, or after volleyball games and dances. "The richness in the Catholic Church is in our differences. We have different ways to talk to God, but we're united in our differences, not separated," said Miguel Harfagar Diaz from Chile, who called his new-found friends "mates in the same faith."

Guzman Carriquiry, undersecretary of the Pontifical Council for the Laity, also praised the diversity of the forum delegates. "The real experience of the forum was that of belonging to the real Catholic Church. That's our strength, our unity," he said. "Here from all countries we are brothers in faith—that's a miracle."

Leslaw Dietrich from Warsaw, Poland, agreed, saying that the most important aspect of the forum was the "spirit of the universal Church. Wherever people come from, they bring pieces and parts of the whole," he said. Dietrich said he wanted to bring back to Poland "the experience of deeply lived faith, not superficial experiences or the faith of our parents, but the shared experiences of living with God."

Not So Crazy After All

Donna Marie Frazier, a twenty-nine-year-old from Philadelphia, said she had often felt alone in her faith and thought it "seemed crazy to believe in God." Meeting with other Catholics from all over the world changed her outlook. She said it

Opposite page: Young people from Croatia, Chile and Macao become friends over their hot dog lunch at Regis University. Many delegates said that their faith was given a boost not so much from the general sessions and workshops as from talking with people from other countries and sharing stories of faith over meals, or after volleyball games and dances.

A World Youth Day host escorts two International Youth Forum delegates from Italy to their rooms at Regis University in Denver.

> "Christ is knocking very hard at many hearts, looking for young people like you to send into the vineyard where an abundant harvest is ready."

gave her "such a source of strength." She said the forum would not come to an end when the delegates returned home, because they planned to write to each other or at least to pray for one another. As a more definitive result of the forum, she said some delegates had made a decision to join religious life and others planned to give more of themselves in service to others.

These decisions made the delegates ripe for receiving the pope's message during their private Mass with him on August 14. During the Mass at Denver's Cathedral of the Immaculate Conception, the delegates cried and trembled with excitement; they sang and stood on tiptoe to get a good view of the pontiff. Pope John Paul II told the forum delegates that they should not to be afraid to spread the Gospel message, particularly through a special commitment to the priesthood or religious life. "Christ is knocking very hard at many hearts, looking for young people like you to send into the vineyard where an abundant harvest is ready," he said. "Young people need to see the practical relevance of their efforts to meet the real needs of people, especially the poor and neglected," the pope said in his homily. "They should also be able to see that their apostolate belongs fully to the Church's mission in the world." He stressed that members of the Church, young or old, would not be effective evangelizers unless they were convinced that their faith had values to offer the world. After the Mass, the pope spent an hour-and-a-half shaking hands with the forum delegates, and he gave each one a rosary.

Living Stones

The delegates responded to the pope's commission in a letter they composed for the August 15 Mass that concluded World Youth Day. In the letter, read by delegate Tom Eggemeir of Dayton, Ohio, the delegates pledged to be "new evangelizers" and the "living stones of the Church." "We recognize that united with our brothers and sisters we are the Church of today and the Church of tomorrow," said the letter, read before approximately 375,000 people gathered at Cherry Creek State Park. The message to the youth included ideas the delegates had discussed during workshops and general sessions. Eggemeir said one of the greatest challenges in composing the letter was trying to get "two hundred hours of workshops into two minutes." Its message reflected both the diversity and the optimism of the delegates, who said they wanted to speak to the world's youth "not about problems, despair and hatred, but about possibilities, hope and love." The delegates expressed a desire to build a new society of love and to commit themselves to serving "the weakest, the poorest and the most vulnerable among us." They said they needed help in such efforts, calling on pastors to continue to assist them in discovering their vocations and to give them the formation they needed as young Christians. In the letter, the delegates repeated the message many World Youth Day participants had expressed during their five days of activities in Denver, thanking the pope for his encouragement and declaring with confidence that, in Christ, today's young people "can change the world."

"Let's sing a song in French." From left to right: Niriena from Burkina Faso, Natunga Noella from Burundi and Zagre from Burkina Faso let loose with a song after registering for the International Youth Forum at Regis University in Denver.

"God's Really Going to Move Here"

World Youth Day began unofficially long before the young pilgrims met at Denver's Civic Center Park for the August 11 opening Mass. During the early part of the week, youth from around the world began streaming into the city's bus and train stations and Denver's Stapleton International Airport with backpacks, bedrolls and high spirits.

The separate routes these young people took to arrive at the Mile High City converged at McNichols Sports Arena, where they gathered to register for the event scheduled to take place from August 11 to 15. In the arena's parking lot, full of buses and vans, including one van whose back window displayed the soaped-in message "Denver or bust," youth from all around the world set the tone for the upcoming events. Instead of giving in to fatigue from their travels and the frustration of waiting while their group leaders registered them, they started introducing themselves to each other. It did not take long for some of the participants to take out their guitars and play folk songs. Spontaneously, young adults and teens followed a Mexican group's lead, linking arms to dance and sing the hokeypokey in Spanish. Later, Argentineans, Italians and American Samoans formed a snaking conga line around the parking lot. They had no need of words to say that they were having a good time or that they would give the pope a warm welcome when he met with them; their enthusiasm spoke for itself.

Planes, Trains and Automobiles

Each group had its own story of jet lag from overnight flights from the Far East or of car

Above: Even the folks from "St. Joe's" parish of Sharon, Pennsylvania made it out to Denver.

Opposite page: Standing room only. Every square inch of Celebration Plaza was filled for the opening Mass of World Youth Day on August 11, 1993.

trouble from trips across the midwestern states. A California teen who drove a van of World Youth Day participants to Denver said he had sprinkled holy water from Lourdes on his overheated engine and had never had another problem. Teens from New Jersey referred to their three days on the road with matching blue T-shirts that read, "I survived the van ride."

Although most pilgrims arrived by modern transportation, some used more primitive means. A group of twenty-one bicyclists from St. Cloud, Minnesota, pedaled the one-thousand-mile distance in eleven days, staying at church halls along the

"It's cool to be Catholic," World Youth Day delegates were saying. This young woman took the message literally by taking a stroll through the plaza fountain in the heat of the afternoon.

Instead of giving into fatigue from their travels and the frustration of waiting while their group leaders registered them, they started introducing themselves to each other. Later, Argentineans, Italians and American Samoans formed a snaking conga line around the parking lot.

way. Paul Marquis, from Vancouver, Canada, walked, bused, cycled and walked to cover the two thousand miles to reach Denver. "It was a good old-fashioned pilgrimage," he said. "I came for the amendment of my life and to get closer to God.... It's been better than I ever even imagined."

When the young pilgrims finally arrived at their destination, they found their lodgings as diverse as the countries they represented. They stayed in hotels, dorms, convents or with families from local parishes. They camped out in high-school gymnasiums, empty office buildings, parish halls and in Denver's Stock Show Expo Hall. Some groups stayed in winter resorts that were located hours away from Denver and drove into the city each day for the events.

A group of forty-five hundred Italians bunked down in a parking garage of the Auraria College campus in Denver. Although most of these young people were accustomed to student travel, they were not used to cots replacing cars on concrete floors and the $1 fee for the facility's showers. Most of the youth kept their good spirits, however, and affectionately dubbed their lodging "L'Albergo

Country singer Wynnona Judd takes the stage during a kickoff concert for at least 50,000 World Youth Day delegates at Celebration Plaza.

Garage" (the Hotel Garage).

About five hundred Spanish young people stayed in a village of ninety tepees in the mountains west of Denver, responding to an invitation to experience Western heritage. Begona Osborne, who stayed in the tepee village with her group of 106 from the Diocese of Jerez de la Frontera in southern Spain, said she came to World Youth Day "because the pope has congregated young people...to proclaim what we believe in." The young visitors from Spain were going to see an evening of Native American dancing and to take part in a buffalo-meat barbecue. They planned to stay on an

extra week to see the mountains.

The Spaniards were not the only ones planning to delay their return trips. Australian travelers made their stop in Denver part of a pilgrimage trip to missionary sites across the United States, and French pilgrims were planning to visit San Francisco when the papal events were finished.

Others arrived early in order to enjoy the sights of the Rocky Mountains. Bishop J. Keith Symons of Palm Beach, Florida, took a group of 250 teen pilgrims and adult chaperons to Rocky Mountain National Park before World Youth Day events started. He celebrated Mass for the group at

Friends that pray together stay together. A group of delegates takes time out to pray, not an uncommon sight during the World Youth Day events.

the bottom of a ski slope, using a picnic table for an altar and giving a homily about how Jesus and his followers often went to the mountains to pray. After Mass, the bishop joined the Florida teenagers in sliding down the grassy ski slope on pieces of cardboard and throwing snowballs on one of the snow-capped mountain peaks. From the majestic Rocky Mountains to the city streets of Denver, the youth of the world were having a good time in each other's company.

Jammin' with Wynonna!

On the afternoon of August 11 they began piling in to Denver's Civic Center Park, renamed Celebration Plaza for World Youth Day. They listened to musical performances by such artists as country singer Wynonna Judd, who had the young people up on their feet, dancing and singing for ninety minutes.

The grassy park, located between the gold-domed Colorado state capitol and Denver's city government buildings, seemed to be transformed that afternoon to a fairground without rides. Some of the young people jumped in a plaza fountain to cool off in the 88-degree weather. Others lined up at concession and souvenir stands or at the dozens of booths from Catholic organizations selling their wares or looking for new members. The young people also started a custom that would be carried on throughout their Denver stay; they traded mementos such as pins, scarves, pictures or hats, and signed each other's t-shirts.

"It's an awesome experience with all these people of different nationalities gathering,"

Opposite page: They couldn't have done this during ski season! Bishop J. Keith Symons of Palm Beach, Florida, celebrates Mass for a group of pilgrims at the bottom of a Rocky Mountain ski slope.

Clothes are hung out to dry in a tepee village west of Denver where 500 Spanish youths had a taste of the "Wild West" during World Youth Day.

said Connie Texeira, a youth director from St. Benedict's Parish in Kona, Hawaii. "We're hoping we can go back and share the abundant life the pope is talking about and bring back those who have fallen away from the Church," she added. "We're going to go back filled with the Spirit."

"I think it tops the cake…the pope being here," said Jessica Tough of North Bay, Ontario, as she sat with four friends atop a low wall enjoying the plaza activity.

Some youth groups came to the plaza directly from the airport with their suitcases still in tow, including a group of fifteen from Las Vegas who rested against their luggage on the edge of the park. Pauline Villapando, a fifteen-year-old in the

Opposite page: World Youth Day was a colorful meeting of hearts, minds, souls and outerwear.

> **"We're hoping we can go back and share the abundant life the pope is talking about and bring back those who have fallen away from the Church."**

group, said she was surprised at the turnout, because she "didn't think there were so many teenagers who were Catholic."

Great Expectations

Overall, most of the youth were excited to be with the crowd and were looking forward to seeing the pope. Some were not sure what to expect in the

"Um, yes, I'd like to order a pizza with pepperoni, mushrooms and anchovies.... And could you please deliver it to Celebration Plaza?.... I'll be the bishop dressed in white, wearing glasses. Thanks."

Right: "We've got the beat." Young Catholics from Cameroon play native instruments during an impromptu jam session in a Denver park.

five days of activities, but others had high hopes. Lori Covak, from St. Paul, Minnesota, said she believed "a lot of people would turn back to the Church and have a personal relationship with God" during World Youth Day. Her friend, Keith Streifel, from Williston, North Dakota, agreed with her expectations, saying, "God's really gonna move here."

As the Mass was about to begin, the carnival became an open-air cathedral with lots of pageantry. The crowd was greeted in several different languages, and participants waved flags and banners as African drummers drew attention to the stage. Loud bells rang to start the procession of Vietnamese youth with brightly colored kites,

"We are brothers and sisters in the Faith." Energetic young people from all over the world are caught up in the contagious spirit of World Youth Day.

Native American Indian dancers, choir members, youth carrying the World Youth Day cross and hundreds of bishops smiling and waving to the jam-packed crowd.

Main celebrant and homilist Denver Archbishop J. Francis Stafford told the 100,000 youth that they were to be the "leaders of the new millennium" and that they were charged with helping the world turn away from its "love affair" with the power and violence that marked the century. He told them to learn from Pope John Paul II's example to struggle against violence and said the pope's writings, particularly his poetry, could help young people understand more about their faith and deepen their understanding of God.

The archbishop said he hopes the transformation that the youth experience during World Youth Day would "constantly astonish" them. Such astonishment is, he added, "the spirit of childhood" that the Catholic Church must keep alive in the third millennium.

The Church seemed very much alive that night at the park and for several hours into the night in the city streets. Young people literally filled one of the main streets, which had been closed for pedestrians, marching in groups, waving flags of their homelands and singing at the top of their lungs. They gave high-fives to outdoor cafe patrons and greeted each other with cheers.

The youth invasion taking place in Denver was highly energetic and enthusiastic, with a spirit that could not be contained.

Opposite page: The Denver skyline was the highlighted background of Celebration Plaza where youth delegates gathered for the opening Mass.

CHAPTER 8

Rockies Rock in Mile-High Welcome

Teenagers and young adults from all over the world greeted Pope John Paul II with a fever-pitched frenzy on August 12 at Mile High Stadium. The stadium, home to Denver's baseball Rockies and football Broncos, rocked with excitement as ninety thousand youths jumped up and down, waved banners, flags and handkerchiefs, stomped their feet, took flash pictures and wiped their eyes at the thrill of catching a glimpse of the renowned leader of the Catholic Church.

The excitement started long before the pope's helicopter was spotted in the cloudy evening sky and the stadium scoreboard lit up with the words, "Welcome," "Wilkomen," "Bienvenidos" and "Benvenuti." For nearly three hours the World Youth Day participants at the outdoor stadium had been dancing and singing in the rain, in anticipation of greeting the pontiff. Even the bishops sitting together in their own section got into the act by doing the wave with everyone else in the stadium. With arms around each other's shoulders they swayed to the theme song of World Youth Day, "We Are One Body," by Irish-born pop singer Dana.

Banners unfurled down each of the aisles and a large white cross was displayed on the stadium floor as the pope entered the stadium waving and smiling at the crowd. The young people raced to the sides of the field, cameras swinging and arms outstretched, as the pope looped around the stadium track in his white popemobile. They continued to cheer when he got out of the car and walked away from security agents to shake the hands extended to him over the chain-link fence.

A Noisy Explosion

The crowd's exuberance did not wane when Pope John Paul II walked up the platform steps and took the microphone. Scarcely was the pope able to say "Dear young people" before their enthusiasm exploded once again in shouts, cheers, whistles and applause.

Like any good teacher, the pope took roll call of the audience, calling out the names of many of the nearly one hundred countries represented. The participants, sitting in stadium sections with others from their country, shouted and waved banners and flags at the mention of their homeland.

"This World Youth Day has brought us to Denver, a stupendous setting in the heart of the United States of America. I greet each one of you:

Opposite page: "I greet each of you: 'A great multitude which no man could number, from every nation, from all tribes and people and tongues' (Rev 7:9). I greet your bishops, your priests, your spiritual guides, your families. I thank you for being here." Pope John Paul II reaches out to shake the hands extended to him over the chain link fence at the jam-packed stadium.

He's here! Pope John Paul II steps off the plane at Stapleton International Airport in Denver, starting his four-day visit with youths from around the world.

'A great multitude which no man could number, from every nation, from all tribes and peoples and tongues,'" the pope said, quoting the Book of Revelation. The pontiff also addressed individually the various groups in the stadium in more than a dozen languages, including Arabic, Polish, French, Spanish, Italian, German, Swahili, Vietnamese, Portuguese, Russian, Lithuanian and Croatian.

Life...and Lots of It!

"We have come to Denver as pilgrims," he told the crowd in English. "We are continuing the journey made by millions of young people in the previous World Youth Days: to Rome, to Buenos Aires, to Santiago de Compostela, to Czestochowa." The pope commented that this par-

> "Of course we are here to listen to one another: I to you, and you to the pope. But above all we are in Denver to hear the one true word of life—the eternal Word who was in the beginning with God."

ticular World Youth Day did not center around a shrine or place of honor but was instead a pilgrimage to the modern city of Denver, set in the natural surroundings of the Rocky Mountains. "We are therefore searching for the reflection of God not only in the beauty of nature but also in humanity's achievements and in each individual person," he said. "On this pilgrimage our steps are guided by the words of Jesus Christ: `I came that they may have life, and have it abundantly,'" he added, quoting the theme of World Youth Day 1993.

In his forty-five minute address, the pope said his purpose in meeting with the young people that evening was to invite them to enter into the depths of their hearts, "and to live the next few days as a real encounter with Jesus Christ."

"Of course we are here to listen to one another: I to you, and you to the pope. But above all we are in Denver to hear the one true word of life—the eternal Word who was in the beginning with God," he said. "Young people of America and of the world, listen to what Christ the Redeemer is

"Mr. President, dear friends, dear people of America,... The ultimate test of your greatness is the way you treat every human being, but especially the weakest and most defenseless ones. The best traditions of your land presume respect for those who cannot defend themselves. If you want equal justice for all, and true freedom and lasting peace, then, America, defend life! All the great causes that are yours today will have meaning only to the extent that you guarantee the right to life and protect the human person." Good advice! Got that everyone? Mr. Clinton?

saying to you!…World Youth Day challenges you to be fully conscious of who you are as God's dearly beloved sons and daughters," the pope said to applause and cheers that frequently interrupted his speech, even after a steady rain began to fall in the stadium.

The youth, undaunted by the downpour, pulled out umbrellas and brightly colored ponchos or took shelter under the gigantic banners they had made for the occasion. At least forty thousand other World Youth Day participants who were unable to attend the welcome ceremony at the stadium because of seating limitations also braved the rain as they watched the pope's speech from giant television screens at Celebration Plaza. The pope himself responded to the evening shower with a mere "What means the rain?" as he continued his talk.

He told the young people, "Jesus has called each one of you to Denver for a purpose. You must live these days in such a way that when the time comes to return home, each one of you will have a clearer idea of what Christ expects of you. Each one must have the courage to go and spread the good news among the people of the last part of the

"I'll tell you, Mr. President, who *I* think is the greatest saxophone player of all time…." Well, they probably talked about more serious things like world peace, hunger, the right to life, global moral chaos, etc., but since it was a private conversation we'll never know.

Opposite page: A World Youth Day delegate from Ukraine gets in a quick word with the pope at the airport.

World Youth Day delegates sat with members of their country during the welcoming ceremony.

twentieth century, in particular among young people of your own age, who will take the Church and society into the next century."

"A Lot of People are Here. That's Cool."

His message certainly did not fall on deaf ears. Jason Sledd of Decatur, Alabama, thought the pope's words would "increase excitement about the Church." He said he was "awestruck" by the opportunity to shake the pope's hand at the stadium. He also said he liked the pontiff's speech and looked forward to hearing him say Mass.

"It's an honor for us when we're so young to get to listen to the pope in person," said Yvette Stachel, a teen from St. Cecilia Parish in Detroit, who said she came to World Youth Day to expand what she knows about God and her Catholic faith.

T. J. Muniz from Our Lady of Fatima Parish in Grand County, New Mexico, said he, too, was there "to expand my faith a little bit more.... It's fun," he added. "And a lot of people are here. That's cool."

Carlos Romero, a native of El Salvador who lives in New York, said through an interpreter that seeing the pope was "so extraordinary, it's hard to explain the feeling that Jesus Christ is working through the pope."

For some, seeing the vast number of young people was as impressive as seeing the pope. "No rock-and-roll singer could get together so many people," said Peter Nunez of the Dominican

Republic. "Only the work of God could unite so many people. I've never seen so many people and what I'm feeling is I'm not the only one in the Church who is struggling. There is a universal Church." Russ Pryor, a group chaperon from Lewiston, Michigan, said the enthusiasm among the young people showed "there's hope for the world still."

Such hope was expressed in the pope's words and in the faces of the young, but it was also evident for some in the rainbow that appeared over the stadium scoreboard as the pope finished speaking. Sheila McCarron, a chaperon for the Archdiocese of Washington youth group, said the rainbow has often been used in local and national youth conferences as "a symbol of youth, their vitality and their hope."

"Hasta la vista"

The pope apologized for his "long, too long" speech, but the participants did not groan or sigh; they only protested, "No!" as if they were eager to hear more. "With great joy, I look forward to our next meeting. *Hasta la vista!*" he concluded.

The pope's final words came at the end of a long day for him, since he had just arrived that afternoon in Denver from his trip to Mexico, which he had visited after stopping in Jamaica. When he landed at Stapleton International Airport, the pope had received a taste of the welcome he would later get at other World Youth Day events; a few hundred young people had greeted him with shouts of "John Paul II, we love you!" and interrupted his speech with cheers and applause.

At one point the pope had looked up from

Sing it, Dana! Yah! Irish-born Christian singer Dana rallies the crowd with the song she composed especially for World Youth Day, "We Are One Body".

have meaning only to the extent that you guarantee the right to life and protect the human person," he had said. He had added that he had a "special joy" in coming to World Youth Day with "young people gathered from all over the world for a serious reflection on the theme of life: the human life which is God's marvelous gift to each of us, and the transcendent life which Jesus Christ our Savior offers."

The pope had acknowledged some of the sufferings that today's youth experience, such as natural calamities, famines, economic and political crises, wars and the breakdown of families. Despite the struggles of young people, the pope had said many of them are deeply concerned about the world and "ready to give the best of themselves in service to others."

He had also told the assembled crowd that he had come to Denver "to listen to the young people gathered here, to experience their inexhaustible quest for life." And from the emotional reaction of the young people gathered for the welcoming ceremony at Mile High Stadium, it seemed the pope had already received a full dose of what he was seeking.

Opposite page: "It is he, Jesus Christ, the true life, who gives hope and purpose to our earthly existence, opens our minds and hearts to the goodness and beauty of the world around us, to solidarity and friendship with our fellow human beings, to intimate communion with God himself, in a love that goes beyond all limits of time and space, to eternal, unassailable happiness." The pope listens to presentations at Mile High Stadium.

his prepared text and asked the youths, "You are crying for what the pope says or against?" "For!" they responded.

At the airport arrival ceremony, attended by Church leaders, President Clinton and other government officials, the pope had urged Americans to defend life. The pope and president would later meet privately at Regis University.

"All the great causes that are yours today will

Before the Pope speaks to the whole group assembled at Mile High Stadium, he has a private talk with a young man and woman who were there to greet him.

Opposite: "Hasta la vista," Pope John Paul II told the crowd, after apologizing for his "long, too long, speech." The youth continued to cheer as if they were hoping for an encore. "Their response," The Holy Father would tell the bishops the next day, "clearly indicates that they have perceived something of what the eternal Father reveals to the 'the little ones' (cf. Mt 11:25). They are thirsty to know more, to penetrate more deeply into the mystery of Christ and the Church. They know that the Father can open that door to them, just as he revealed the heart of the mystery to Peter at Caesarea Philippi.

CHAPTER 9

The Way of the Cross

Only twenty-four hours after the foot-stomping revelry took place at Mile High Stadium, the athletic field was transformed into a solemn arena of prayer for the Way of the Cross. On August 13, the green baseball diamond that had been filled with young people during the pope's welcoming ceremony was empty except for those leading the Stations of the Cross, which were set up as simple markers along the field's perimeter. Cardinal Eduardo Pironio, president of the Pontifical Council for the Laity, led the stations, accompanied by eight torch bearers and ten youths holding aloft the official World Youth Day cross.

A hushed crowd of about seventy thousand watched and prayed from their stadium seats as the cardinal walked to each station commemorating the passion and death of Jesus. Prayers were read in English, Spanish, French, Italian and Polish from the stage at the south end of the stadium. Brother Roger Schutz of the Taizé ecumenical community in France and Sr. Raphaella, a member of Mother Teresa's Missionaries of Charity, gave reflections, while a mime troupe, Fountain Square Fools from Cincinnati, acted out each station.

In a live message broadcast on the scoreboard screen at the end of the three-hour Stations, Pope John Paul II told the young people that the Way of the Cross had led them to the "heart of the mystery of God's redeeming love," which he called the center of the Church's life and the "core of all Christian witness and teaching."

"There is much to think and pray about," he said, urging the youth to "take courage in the face of life's difficulties," and to commit themselves to the struggle for justice, solidarity and peace in the world. "Offer your youthful energies and your talents to building a civilization of Christian love. Be witnesses of God's love for the innocent and the weak, for the poor and oppressed."

The pope also urged the young people to build on the "moment of intensity" they had reached in their World Youth Day experience by finding time for quiet reflection and taking advantage of the sacrament of penance offered by many of the priests during World Youth Day. "In the name of Christ, in the name of the Church, in the

Opposite page: " The Way of the Cross has led you to the heart of the mystery of God's redeeming love, the mystery which is at the center of the Church's life, the mystery which is the core of all Christian witness and teaching. There is much to think and pray about." With arms outstretched, youth delegates hoist the cross during the Stations.

Busloads of young people make their way to Mile High Stadium for the Way of the Cross.

name of needy humanity: I encourage you to have that new life in you! Be witnesses of that new life to the world around you," he emphasized.

The youth responded to the pope's message with respectful applause, not with the shouting and cheering they had given him on his arrival. They spoke with seriousness about giving their lives in service to others as Christ had done, and they said that they too had crosses to bear in today's world, such as peer pressure and loneliness.

World Youth Day delegates did not have to look far for a good example in scheduling quiet time for prayer. The pope himself had spent most of August 13 hiking, relaxing and praying at Camp St. Malo, a 160-acre archdiocesan mountainside retreat seventy miles north of Denver.

"Soul Scrubbing"

Nor did the youth have to look far for priests to hear their confessions. Impromptu "confessionals" had been set up, and were frequently used, in stadium seats, under trees at Celebration

World Youth Day delegates stick together by forming a human chain as they walk into Mile High Stadium.

"I hope that you will avail yourselves of the many priests who are here. In the sacrament of penance they are ambassadors to you of Christ's loving forgiveness." In a typical scene during World Youth Day, a young man receives the sacrament of reconciliation at an impromptu "confessional" at the Colorado Convention Center.

Plaza and in their traditional location, local churches. At least one thousand youth daily went to Denver's Holy Ghost Church, open twenty-four hours a day for perpetual adoration. Father Peter Armenio, an Opus Dei priest from Chicago, made sure there were enough priests to hear confessions at all hours and in several languages. "We have nonstop confessions throughout the night," he said, calling the turnout a "tangible and powerful sign that young people are searching for something spiritual and transcendent. They are saying they want Catholicism. They want to be spiritual, and they want to be challenged," he added.

During the middle of the day on August 13, the line of young people waiting outside the confessionals looked like one of the food lines at Denver's festive Celebration Plaza, where many of the World Youth Day events were taking place.

But the similarity ended there, because inside the church the young people were silent. They put their backpacks beside them as they knelt and prayed in the pews. Some bowed their heads in prayer, others read prayer books or clutched rosaries. Instead of listening to talks or musicians, the young people knelt quietly before the Blessed Sacrament, which had been placed on an altar adorned at the sides with flickering votive candles.

Youth from all parts of the world had signed up to come to the church all during the day and night. Lynn Mojica from Boston said she had come to go to confession. The opportunity to pray in the quiet church "gave meaning to everything else that's going on," she said. "It's what's important."

"It's a very good place for refreshment,"

Wearing new white sneakers with gold shoelaces given to him by a youth delegate, Pope John Paul II hikes beside a mountain stream during his day of relaxation at Camp St. Malo, near Estes Park, Colorado.

A group of young women pose for the camera before taking part in the solemn Way of the Cross.

added Jane Njoroge from Worcester, Massachusetts.

Father Armenio said the young people had not spoken to him about what it meant for them to go to confession or to pray, but he said they didn't need to. "I can see it in their eyes."

The faith of the young people could also be seen in the sacrifices they made. At the pope's suggestion, many of them decided to give up their midday meal on Friday and donate the money they had saved to St. Joseph's Hospital in Kitovu, Uganda, a hospital that treats AIDS patients.

Others practiced their faith by devoting their time on August 12 and 13 to service projects such as building homes, cleaning Denver's parks and recreation areas, visiting hospitals and nursing homes, taking part in a canned food drive and sorting and packing food for the needy.

Helping build homes for low-income families

is faith in action, said Lisa Johnson, a youth from Lansing, Michigan, who volunteered to help Habitat for Humanity, a nonprofit Christian housing ministry, to put up four one-story, four-bedroom homes in a Denver neighborhood. "Being Catholic to me is helping other people who need help, children and families who just need a place to live," said Lisa, sixteen, a member of St. Gerard Parish. "We're supposed to help people, and we're here doing it."

Lisa and the other Lansing youth joined about

> **"Offer your youthful energies and your talents to building a civilization of Christian love. Be witness of God's love for the innocent and the weak, for the poor and oppressed."**

two hundred World Youth Day delegates in Habitat's project. Doug Moore, St. Gerard's youth coordinator, said the work fit the young people's commitment for World Youth Day, which was to "make a difference, make an impact" on people's lives.

Maria de la Torre, a single mother of four, said she felt "up in the clouds" with her new home. "It's really an indescribable feeling. It's elation." She said the youths' involvement in the project "shows that young people really care."

The youth delegates had plenty of opportunities to act on their faith, but they also had their faith nourished during daily catechetical sessions held at several sites around the city for various age groups and languages. Each of the three sessions focused on a theme and included the sacrament of

> Young people spoke with seriousness about giving their lives in service to others as Christ had done, and they said that they too had crosses to bear in today's world, such as peer pressure and loneliness.

reconciliation, community building, a Scripture reading, a lesson by a bishop and witness by a youth.

Bishop Charles J. Chaput of Rapid City, South Dakota, who led the youth during one of the sessions, told them to "live the

Prior to the Way of the Cross ceremony, two delegates from Guam have their hands full with flags and a banner.

Cardinal Eduardo Pironio, president of the Pontifical Council for the Laity, leads the world's youth through the Stations of the Cross at Mile High Stadium.

Gospel without excuse. Live it radically, simply and plainly, and make it clear for others." In an interview, the bishop said he felt renewed by "the faith and energy of these young people," which showed him the Church has a "strength we don't even know we have."

Each bishop also met with the young people of his diocese for question-and-answer sessions. Archbishop William H. Keeler of Baltimore answered questions on subjects ranging from the topic of ordination to what the pope was really like. He challenged the Baltimore youths to take their enthusiasm back to their parishes, saying "You can do a better job than I in telling what it's

like to go on pilgrimage in the one body of Christ."

Cardinal James A. Hickey of Washington invited the youth delegates to meet with him in the fall for a "reunion" in which they could come up with suggestions on how "we can best go forward together."

Many of the young people who attended these sessions said they liked having the opportunity to meet their bishops and to talk with them. The words and challenges these young Catholics had already heard in only their first few days in Denver made the pope's words at the Way of the Cross, "there is much to think and pray about," certainly ring true.

Opposite page: "I invite you to create a climate of silence and reflection, so that a deepening awareness of the mystery can grow in every young person gathered here. Let us pray that the love which God pours into our hearts through the Holy Spirit (cf. Rom 5:5) may not be blocked or hindered by passing distractions." A young woman prayerfully watches the Way of the Cross.

"Backpacks Are Our Cross"

The words of Jesus "pick up your mat and walk" were taken to heart by about sixty thousand World Youth Day participants. On August 14, they picked up their backpacks, sleeping bags, duffel bags and water bottles to walk the fifteen-mile pilgrimage to Cherry Creek State Park, where they would attend an evening prayer vigil and stay overnight for Sunday's Mass.

The young people had begun their pilgrimage prayerfully with a morning Mass at Celebration Plaza. In the homily, Auxiliary Bishop Robert F. Morneau of Green Bay, Wisconsin, made several allusions to the Christian journey. "Let us go together. The road is long and calls for companions," he said. He also spoke of famous biblical roads, the road to Emmaus, Saul's road to Damascus and the road taken by Isaiah the prophet. Like Isaiah, the young pilgrims would be asked "Whom shall we send? Who will go into the world to be a light in the darkness, to bring peace into a world of injustice and to bring hope?" Isaiah responded, "Lord, here I am, send me," and so should you, the bishop said. "We are challenged to respond." Fittingly, the pilgrims responded with shouts and cheers when the bishop told them to begin their pilgrimage "in the peace of Christ."

As they left downtown Denver for the park, they were led by a group of young Philippine pilgrims carrying the official World Youth Day cross. Youth from around the world filled the pilgrimage route with banners, flags, high spirits and songs.

The differences between the backgrounds and homelands of the pilgrims seemed to disappear as they made their way along the same path to the site where they would meet the rest of the World Youth Day participants and the pope who had called them all together. Some used walking sticks, a few pushed wheelchairs or shopping carts piled high with gear for their overnight camp, and still others carried their belongings hobo style—holding the end of a long stick with their backpack slung across it.

Along the way, pilgrims gathered around someone with a guitar or ukelele to sing traditional folk tunes or religious songs. Others prayed the Rosary or just talked and made new acquaintances. A few groups formed a human chain, holding hands as they walked the bike path, almost as much for moral support for the trek ahead as for keeping track of one another.

"We're talking and praying. It will help strengthen my faith," said Carroll Bright, a youth from Grapevine, Texas. "I'm learning about other people, other cultures, and finding out how much more similar we are than different."

Opposite page: "Our backpacks are our cross," a youth said, describing the trek where everyone carried backpacks, sleeping bags, bedrolls and water bottles along the bike path route. Some of the pilgrims went farther than comparing their walk to the road to Calvary: they offered to carry each other's heavy backpacks, comparing their actions to that of Simon of Cyrene when he helped carry the cross for Jesus.

Slurrp! Slurrp! Slurrp! Who needs a cup? A thirsty pilgrim gets a refreshing drink of water at a stop along the way. At aid stations and the backyards of friendly Denver residents, the walkers were never too far from a drink to keep them going.

Thank you, Denver!

The pilgrims were also a visible witness of faith to Denver onlookers. Signs on residents' homes along the route welcomed the youth, and many of the locals came out to greet them. On one street overpass, thirty people stretched across to greet walkers. At another spot, five elderly women from a nearby nursing home sat in lawn chairs to watch the pilgrims.

"I'm not a Catholic, and to a cynical old lawyer like me this is just wonderful," said Denver resident Jerry Valentine, who said he was impressed by the excitement and enthusiasm of the pilgrims whom he saw firsthand when he handed them water.

Paul Spaeth, a member of Christ the King Parish in Denver who greeted walkers from an overpass, said World Youth Day offered a "renewal of spirit" and a time of healing for the city, which had experienced a summer of gang violence and other crimes.

The waves, cheers and drinks from garden hoses were well received by the pilgrims. "We appreciate (that) the people from Colorado are pushing us on. Everybody has a smile, is greeting us, giving us water," said Henry Smith, a group chaperon from Winslow, Arizona. He described the fifteen-mile hike as more than a walk. "It's all about knowing Jesus Christ, about meeting people, having a journey. It's all about building up the faith."

Many of the walkers were equally determined. At aid stations along the way, offering water and bananas, some young pilgrims just paused to take their refreshment and then kept walking. Others collapsed on the grass for a moment, resting against their heavily laden backpacks and talking about their aching feet.

Aid stations were the place where the World Youth Day cross was transferred from pilgrims from one country to those of another to carry. The cross, held aloft and leading the way, served as a constant reminder to the pilgrims of the spiritual significance of their trek. But the young people who were miles behind the cross did not need reminders of why they were there. "This experience is so moving," said Chris Keppler from Parma, Ohio. "It's not some kind of vacation. It's a religious retreat, and I came for a purpose. The pilgrimage is like the road that Jesus took to Calvary. Our backpacks are our cross."

A Time for Reflection

Christine Leando from San Jose, California, also said the walk made her think of how Jesus felt while he carried his cross. "There are times I've felt like stumbling, but I have my friends to pick me up. This has made me think a lot about my faith, what I do, how I show it around me. It's neat to let other people know what your faith is. I feel I was really meant to walk this."

Some of the pilgrims went farther than comparing their walk to the road to Calvary: they offered to carry each other's heavy backpacks, comparing their actions to that of Simon of Cyrene when he carried the cross for Jesus.

The journey was not such an unusual sacrifice for everyone. Youth from Sudan, for example,

"I'm not a Catholic, and to a cynical old lawyer like me this is just wonderful."

said they were used to walking such distances every day. Neither was it an unending excursion. Four hours after the pilgrims began, the first group caught sight of their destination, a wide field against the backdrop of the Rocky Mountains. As they neared the site, many spontaneously began dancing and singing.

Teresa Piras, from Columbus, Ohio, said she didn't originally plan on making the pilgrimage. "It's something I never thought I would do, but this whole experience has brought me closer to who I am and where I stand in my faith," she said. "I can't believe this is really happening."

The walk ended on a high road overlooking the vigil site. From late morning until dusk, pilgrims snaked down the road into Cherry Creek State Park, land that is usually home to deer, rabbits, coyote, hawks and owls.

Other World Youth Day participants, who were not able to make the whole pilgrimage because of space limitations, were not exempt from walking. Buses dropped them off in locations up to five miles away from the park.

As they converged on the dusty field, they took their assigned places in roped-off sections. Missouri youth unrolled their sleeping bags near Australians in cowboy hats serenading them with songs such as "Waltzing Matilda," and Italian youth set up their jam-packed "camp" near their neighbors at home, the French. In each section of the park, groups and individuals had their own stories of struggles and triumphs of faith. Members of a group of 126 Irish youth used expressions that were typical of most World Youth Day delegates in describing their Denver experience: "brilliant, fantastic, unreal, awesome."

Liam Mullholland, a twenty-one-year-old

Sudanese youth take a turn carrying the World Youth Day cross during the last leg of the 15-mile pilgrimage to Cherry Creek State Park. Apparently the trek was no endurance test for the hardy Sudanese who said that they often walk such distances every day! No problem!

Howdy, Pilgrims! European scouts are geared up for World Youth Day adventure. As they will tell you, always be prepared...to share your faith!

from Belfast, Northern Ireland, also reiterated the familiar phrase, that World Youth Day was "an experience of a lifetime." His background, however, was not like everyone else's in that dusty field. On his street at home, he said, five Catholics had been shot dead in the fighting that has killed more than three thousand people since it began twenty-four years ago.

"Faith is in a crisis in Belfast, especially with youth. Their parents and grandparents have grown up with troubles, and they've lost any hope they ever had," he said. But Liam would not go home hopeless. He said the experience of being with so many other believers in Denver gave him "a bit of hope in the midst of the violence" he sees daily. "It fills me with hope because I know I'm not alone in my faith."

Gabriel Wurz, a twenty-two-year-old from Monte Carlo, Monaco, said many young people in his country did not struggle with violence or economic hardships but with "nice lives." "The difficulty then," he said, "is people think they don't need God and say, 'Why should I practice my faith?'" He said it was important to make a pilgrimage like this one "to take time out of your life for a few days and to say, 'Where am I with my faith?'" It was also important for him to see he was not alone. "Here I can make a complete circle and see Catholics all around me who share my faith."

The Courage to Believe

And by dusk, just as a smattering of rain fell on them, the sea of young pilgrims, numbering

Enthusiastic young people experience the thrill of meeting the Holy Father face to face and literally cry for joy.

During reverent moments of the vigil, some delegates close their eyes in prayer, others hold candles.

Left: Vigil participants clap, raise their arms and look around at the people of various backgrounds and nationalities.

about 250,000, had stretched to the horizon. And by the time the man of the hour, Pope John Paul II, arrived, a brilliant sunset had broken through the clouds, casting a dramatic glow on both the pilgrims and the Rocky Mountain backdrop behind him.

The pilgrims enthusiastically waved flags, hats and bandannas to greet their spiritual leader as he climbed the steps to the altar on a stage that was nearly the size of a football field. For many, the pontiff was a tiny figure in white in the distance. But he was brought closer by huge television screens positioned throughout the park and by the

A World Youth Day delegate carries a torch during the vigil procession.

> **"I ask you to have the courage to commit yourselves to the truth. Have the courage to believe the good news about life which Jesus teaches in the Gospel."**

sound of his voice, as he switched back and forth between languages, urging and challenging youth to be faithful to the Gospel message.

For twenty-five minutes the pope addressed the young people, speaking sternly at times but also with compassion. "Here this evening, in Cherry Creek State Park in Denver, you represent the youth of the world, with all the questions which the young people at the end of the twentieth century have a need and a right to ask," he said. "In the midst of all of life's contradictions, we search for life's true meaning."

The pope urged the youths, some of whom were listening to his talk through radio translations, to continue to ask and search for meaning and to realize the true answer in Christ. "I ask you to have the courage to commit yourselves to the truth. Have the courage to believe the good news about life which Jesus teaches in the Gospel," he said, to cheers and applause. The pope spoke strongly about destructive forces against life, particularly the "anti-life mentality" which he said is hostile "to life in the womb and life in its last stages." "Abortion and euthanasia—the actual killing of another human being—are hailed as 'rights' and solutions to 'problems,'" he said, thus making God's gift of life "just one more commodity to be organized, commercialized and manipulated according to convenience."

Opposite page: In response to the frequent shouts of "John Paul II, we love you!" from the crowd of over 250,000, the Holy Father replies, "Young people, Pope John Paul II...he loves *you!*"

The pope said that while Christ wants each person to have abundant life, "he sees so many young people throwing away their lives in a flight into irresponsibility and falsehood" through drug and alcohol abuse, pornography, sexual disorders and violence. He cautioned the young men and women to value their lives and not to give in to a "widespread false morality." He urged them to use their conscience, "the most secret core and sanctuary of a person, where we are alone with God," in order to guide their moral decisions. "Only by listening to the voice of God in your most intimate being, and by acting in accordance with its directions, will you reach the freedom you yearn for," he said.

> "Only by listening to the voice of God in your most intimate being, and by acting in accordance with its directions, will you reach the freedom you yearn for."

Although the pope did not mince words, he did not speak down to his young audience or leave them without hope. He told them that against all the "forces of death" in today's world and "in spite of all the false teachers, Jesus Christ continues to offer

"Are we having a great time, or what?!" A group of young people clap and sing in preparation for the Pope's arrival at Cherry Creek State Park.

"I just hope I don't get my face stepped on during the night!" A young man gets his stuff together and shares this common concern with about 250,000 other World Youth Day slumber-party participants.

humanity the only true and realistic hope." He also told them that today's Church needs their involvement because each person has a role to play in building up the body of Christ.

While the pope spoke, young people huddled in groups or under sleeping bags to keep warm in the cool mountain air. Some strained to hear over the noise made by people walking back and forth. Others looked at the World Youth Day prayer book by the light of floodlights or their own flashlights. A few held votive candles aloft.

In closing, the pope prayed to God that he would teach young people "to carry on the vast mission of making you known to all those who have not yet heard of you! Give these young people the courage and generosity of the great missionaries of the past so that, through the witness of their faith

and their solidarity with every brother and sister in need, the world may discover the truth, the goodness and the beauty of the life you alone can give."

Although he barely looked up from his prepared text during his talk, he addressed the gathering informally before he left the stage. "Young people of Denver, Pope John Paul II, he loves you," he said, in response to the frequent shouts he heard of "John Paul II, we love you!"

Looking at his watch, the pope said, "He hopes to meet you tomorrow, and for the moment he says to all of you good night. Make it a night of prayer," he told the pilgrims as they prepared to spend the night under the stars. "Make it a night...of singing, of joy, of sacred joy. Pope John Paul II waits for you tomorrow, the same place. We shall celebrate the great solemnity of Our Lady. *Adios!*"

CHAPTER 11

"Be Proud of the Gospel"

"In the name of Jesus Christ and his Blessed Mother, I say to you…good morning!" was the Holy Father's Sunday greeting to Pilgrims—very few of whom had had any sleep. Perhaps it was the excitement of being at a slumber party with 250,000 friends and the overwhelming desire to meet as many of them as possible. Or maybe it was the way the floodlights brightened the field throughout the night, or the fact that the young pilgrims were packed like sardines on the cold ground, obstacles to anyone who tried to hop over them.

Neulina Morales, a twenty-one-year-old from Guatemala City, said she slept for a half-hour, from 1 to 1:30 a.m., before being awakened by a group who passed by shouting, "Guatemala, Guatemala, get up!" It was as if the excitement of the moment was too good to pass up. Pilgrims could sleep at home; it was not every night that they could mingle with people of their own age and faith from all over the world. So they were unconcerned about the time of night or day. With each passing hour, they prayed, sang, danced and continued to make new friends.

For many who finally did succumb to sleep, the wake-up call, "Good morning pilgrims!" over the loudspeaker in four languages at 5:20 a.m., came a little too soon. As the sun started to rise over the 160-acre field, early risers could be seen walking on tiptoe through a maze of bodies that covered most of the soft, bare ground of Cherry Creek State Park. Others, already awakened by the cold air, dug deeper into their blankets or poked their heads out of their sleeping bags, their hair matted and eyes squinting. Some got ready for "church" that morning by splashing water on their faces or brushing grass from their hair. Women applied makeup or braided each other's hair, and an Air Force cadet shaved with a battery operated razor.

At 6:30 a.m., the billboard-sized television screens blinked to life, and the stacks of stereo speakers crackled with the first sounds of music for the day. Within a half-hour, World Youth Day workers were asking the pilgrims to roll up their sleeping bags to make room for the 125,000 others that were to join them by the time Mass started.

A Hot Time

The Sunday Mass, celebrating the Feast of the Assumption, differed from usual Sunday services primarily because the congregation members were drinking water and sometimes eating popsicles during the ceremony to keep their cool under the blazing sun and dry mountain air. Many of

Opposite page: Preparing to celebrate Mass, Pope John Paul II walks to the altar in his vestments.

those who did not heed the warnings to drink extra water were among the 14,000 treated that day for symptoms of dehydration. Ushers did not busy themselves trying to find seats for Mass-goers. Instead, they cleared paths so that golf carts could take paramedics through the crowd to pilgrims who needed emergency care. Special water lines and faucets had been set up in the park, and tents at the fringes of the crowd sold bottled water. As the morning drew on and temperatures rose into the 90s, people on the backs of pickup trucks threw bottled water to thirsty participants, and a fire truck hosed down pilgrims on the sidelines during the pope's homily.

The pontiff, dressed in traditional vestments that must have been more than a little warm, made no mention of the heat in his thirty-minute homily, although he did shorten his original text. His words to the young pilgrims resounded and further emphasized the call to proclaim the Gospel message that he had given them the previous night. He

Some got ready for "church" that morning by splashing water on their faces or brushing grass from their hair.

did not urge them to prepare for future leadership in the Church and the world but to make their presence felt now.

"At this stage of history, the liberating message of the Gospel of life has been put into your hands. And the mission of proclaiming it to the ends of the earth is now passing to your generation," he said to cheers and applause from the tired but exhilarated pilgrims. "Young pilgrims, Christ needs you to enlighten the world and to show it the 'path of life,'" he added. "Do not be afraid to go out on the streets and into public places, like the first apostles who preached Christ and the good news of salvation in the squares of cities, towns and villages," he said. "This is no time to be

"Hey, anybody happen to know where those crazy Guatemalans are?" Prior to Sunday's Mass and after a night of limited sleep, the Guatemalan delegates pose by their banner in the field at Cherry Creek State Park.

Looking out of the helicopter window with rosary in hand, Pope John Paul II scans the awaiting crowd assembled at Cherry Creek State Park for Assumption Sunday's Mass.

ashamed of the Gospel."

He clearly spelled out the urgency of the youths' mission, saying, "so much depends on you," and "woe to you if you do not succeed in defending life." He also told them, "Christ needs laborers ready to work in his vineyard. May you, the Catholic young people of the world, not fail him."

Although the pope put out a strong call to the young people, he seemed certain

> **"Do not be afraid to break out of comfortable and routine modes of living, in order to take up the challenge of making Christ known in the modern 'metropolis.' "**

they would be able to respond. "I am confident that you have grasped the scale of the challenge that lies before you and that you will have the wisdom and courage to meet that challenge," he said. He asked them to commit their energies, enthusiasm and youthful ideals "to make the Gospel of life penetrate the fabric of society, transforming people's hearts and the structures of society."

He insisted the world needed the message of life in Christ now more than ever, particularly to counter the "culture-of-death" mentality he said was so pervasive. "In our own century, as at no other time in history, 'the culture of death' has assumed a social and institutional form of legality to justify the most horrible crimes against humanity: genocide, 'final solutions,' 'ethnic cleansings,' and the massive 'taking of lives of human beings even before they are born, or before they reach the natural point of death,'" he said in his prepared

A pensive young woman holds aloft a crucifix amid the many banners and flags in the park.

Left: "I've got my headdress, and you've got yours. I like it!" The Pope with crucifix in hand greets Native Americans.

remarks. Those who believe in Christ and live the Gospel must defend human life despite the huge challenges the modern world presents, he added.

The pope said that the work of proclaiming the Gospel could not be done without effort. In fact, he told the youth not to "be afraid to break out of comfortable and routine modes of living, in order to take up the challenge of making Christ known in the modern 'metropolis.'"

Many of the pilgrims had already had a taste of what it meant to break away from comfortable living after driving for days, walking for miles, sleeping on the cold ground (if they slept at all), waiting in line for food or to use the portable toilets

A young man gets a better picture of the pope from atop a friend's shoulders.

and not finding any shady relief from the sun.

"It's worth it!" said a group of teenage girls from the midwestern United States, filling up their water bottles during Mass in front of the McDonald's stand for the third time that morning. "It's awesome. So many people came," chimed in Becky Gentrup of Hartington, Nebraska. "It supports us and helps our faith."

Across the board, it seemed the minor inconveniences these youths experienced did not take away from the significance of meeting the pope and hundreds of thousands of others, nor did it blur their vision of what they were called to do when they returned home.

The closing Mass, ending the five days in

"Life Is Short, Pray Hard."

Denver, was hardly a finale. The pope himself called the World Youth Day celebration only a stop along the way for the youths' life-long pilgrimage as apostles. Nor did he let any opportunity go by to stress the work that lay ahead for these pilgrims. At the end of his sermon, the pope went back to the microphone to say he wanted to make a correction. The pope told the pilgrims that, instead of saying, "You should not be ashamed of the Gospel," he should have said, "You should be proud of the Gospel."

In typical fashion, they expressed their approval through cheers and shouts. Perhaps it was because in five days they had learned what it meant to be proud of their faith. They walked around Denver's parks and city streets proclaiming messages emblazoned on their T-shirts, such as "100 percent Catholic" or "Life Is Short, Pray Hard." Many said that for the first time they were not ashamed of their faith; they could talk about it or sing about it openly. They also realized their faith was not only to be put on for Sunday Mass and then forgotten.

Father Pat Cassalenvovo, a Missionary Father of St. Charles, living in Melbourne, Australia, said the enthusiasm of the youth told him that "the Church is going to be in great hands in the future.... This is the best example of unity in the Church and world unity; these young people have it," he added enthusiastically.

Some, like Martha Arias, a nineteen-year-old from Pasadena, California, said the five days in Denver were more than just a whirlwind of excitement. They were the "foundation to build on." Therese Currie, a twenty-six-year-old from Detroit, agreed. "There is so much here that's not just emotional. The pope said it's great to be excited, but now we have to transform the world." The

Pope John Paul II elevates the chalice as he celebrates Mass on Sunday, August 15, 1993.

A youth delegate has a private moment with the pope.

transformation might have to begin in little ways, such as not being "ashamed to mention Christ in the workplace," said Michelle Mendoza, a twenty-six-year-old from Crown Point, Indiana. Many of the youth said they were inspired to keep up the pace the Holy Father had called them to, because, as Gabriel Wurz from Monaco said, "during a pilgrimage you move, so when you come back you still have the impetus to keep moving."

And many of the pilgrims literally had to keep moving, because they had hours and days of travel left in their return trips. So they exchanged addresses and took snapshots without lingering long on the dusty field after the four-hour Mass had ended. They hoisted backpacks on their shoulders that were covered with mementos from the new friends they had met: small pins such as an Australian koala bear, an Idaho potato, a Spanish Madonna, a Canadian flag or a Vermont skier. Other reminders of their stay included the signatures collected on their T-shirts, sore muscles and, for some, a desire for a shower and home-cooked food.

With souvenirs and memories in tow, they would leave the city they had temporarily transformed to try and do the same in their own homes, neighborhoods, high schools, colleges or workplaces. They could not help but leave motivated by the spirit of the event and the image of hundreds of thousands of young people who shared their beliefs.

"With my testimony, with my life, I will try to express this [World Youth Day] experience," Neulina Morales said. "The pope said we are the Church, and we must act now because we are in the world. I think we can make a difference if we want. We have problems that are big, but we can change them because we have the spirit that the pope transmits."

Opposite page: And now we bid a fond farewell. After four days of participating in World Youth Day events, Pope John Paul II walks to the airplane with Archbishop J. Francis Stafford of Denver (left) and Archbishop William H. Keeler of Baltimore behind him. The Holy Father's last words before leaving: "My gratitude becomes an ardent prayer for the people of this great country, for the fulfillment of America's destiny as one nation under God, with liberty and justice for all. America, defend life so that you may live in peace and harmony. God bless America! God bless you all!"

CHAPTER 12

Words To Live By

Arrival at Stapleton International Airport
August 12

Mr. President,
Dear friends,
Dear people of America,

1. I greatly appreciate your generous words of welcome. The World Youth Day being celebrated this year in Denver gives me the opportunity to meet you and, through you, to express once again to the American people my sentiments of deep esteem and friendship. I thank you and Mrs. Clinton for your kind gesture in coming here personally to welcome me.

I take this opportunity to greet the other representatives of the federal government, of the State of Colorado and of the City of Denver who are present here and to thank all those who have contributed in any way to preparing this visit. I am grateful to the bishops of the United States for their part in organizing the eighth World Youth Day and, in particular, to Archbishop Stafford of Denver and the Catholic Church in Colorado for serving as the local hosts for this important international event.

I am aware that the United States is suffering greatly from the recent flooding in the Midwest. I have felt close to the American people in their tragedy and have prayed for the victims. I invoke almighty God's strength and comfort upon all who have been affected by this calamity.

2. There is a special joy in coming to America for the celebration of this World Youth Day. A nation which is itself still young according to historical standards is hosting young people gathered from all over the world for a serious reflection on the theme of life: the human life which is God's marvelous gift to each one of us and the transcendent life which Jesus Christ our savior offers to those who believe in his name.

I come to Denver to listen to the young people gathered here, to experience their inexhaustible quest for life. Each successive World Youth Day has been a confirmation of young people's openness to the meaning of life as a gift received, a gift to which they are eager to respond by striving for a better world for themselves and their fellow human beings. I believe that we would correctly interpret their deepest aspirations by saying that what they ask is that society—especially the leaders of nations and all who control the destinies of peoples—accept them as true partners in the construction of a more humane, more just, more compassionate world. They ask to be able

to contribute their specific ideas and energies to this task.

3. The well-being of the world's children and young people must be of immense concern to all who have public responsibilities. In my pastoral visits to the Church in every part of the world I have been deeply moved by the almost universal conditions of difficulty in which young people grow up and live. Too many sufferings are visited upon them by natural calamities, famines, epidemics, by economic and political crises, by the atrocities of wars. And where material conditions are at least adequate, other obstacles arise, not the least of which is the breakdown of family values and stability. In developed countries, a serious moral crisis is already affecting the lives of many young people, leaving them adrift, often without hope, and conditioned to look only for instant gratification. Yet everywhere there are young men and women deeply concerned about the world around them, ready to give the best of themselves in service to others and particularly sensitive to life's transcendent meaning.

But how do we help them? Only by instilling a high moral vision can a society ensure that its young people are given the possibility to mature as free and intelligent human beings, endowed with a robust sense of responsibility to the common good, capable of working with others to create a community and a nation with a strong moral fiber. America was built on such a vision, and the American people possess the intelligence and will to meet the challenge of rededicating themselves with renewed vigor to fostering the truths on which this country was founded and by which it grew. Those truths are enshrined in the Declaration of Independence, the Constitution and the Bill of Rights, and they still today receive a broad consensus among Americans. Those truths sustain values which have led people all over the world to look to America with hope and respect.

4. To all Americans, without exception, I present this invitation: Let us pause and reason together (cf. Is 1:18). To educate without a value system based on truth is to abandon young people to moral confusion, personal insecurity and easy manipulation. No country, not even the most powerful, can endure if it deprives its own children of this essential good. Respect for the dignity and worth of every person, integrity and responsibility, as well as understanding, compassion and solidarity toward others, survive only if they are passed on in families, in schools and through the communications media.

America has a strong tradition of respect for the individual, for human dignity and human rights. I gladly acknowledged this during

> "To educate without a value system based on truth is to abandon young people to moral confusion, personal insecurity and easy manipulation. No country, not even the most powerful, can endure if it deprives its own children of this essential good."

my previous visit to the United States in 1987, and I would like to repeat today the hope I expressed on that occasion:

America, you are beautiful and blessed in so many ways.... But your best beauty and your richest blessing is found in the human person: in each man, woman and child, in every immigrant, in every native-born son and daughter.... The ultimate test of your greatness is the way you treat every human being, but especially the weakest and most defenseless ones. The best traditions of your land presume respect for those who cannot defend themselves. If you want equal justice for all, and true freedom and lasting peace, then, America, defend life! All the great causes that are yours today will have meaning only to the extent that you guarantee the right to life and protect the human person (Departure speech in Detroit, September 19, 1987).

5. Mr. President, my reference to the moral truths which sustain the life of the nation is not without relevance to the privileged position which the United States holds in the international community. In the face of tensions and conflicts that too many peoples have endured for so long—I am thinking in particular of the Middle East region and some African countries—and in the new situation emerging from the events of 1989—especially in view of the tragic conflicts now going on in the Balkans and in the Caucasus—the international community ought to establish more effective structures for maintaining and promoting justice and peace. This implies that a concept of strategic interest should evolve which is based on the full development of peoples—out of poverty and toward a more dignified existence, out of injustice and exploitation toward fuller respect for the human person and the defense of universal human rights. If the United Nations and other international agencies, through the wise and honest cooperation of their member nations, succeed in effectively defending stricken populations, whether victims of underdevelopment or conflicts or the massive violation of human rights, then there is indeed hope for the future. For peace is the work of justice.

6. The bounty and providence of God have laid an enormous responsibility on the people and government of the United States. But that burden is also the opportunity for true greatness. Together with millions of people around the globe I share the profound hope that in the present international situation the United States will spare no effort in advancing authentic freedom and in fostering human rights and solidarity.

May God guide this nation, and keep alive in it—for endless generations to come—the flame of liberty and justice for all. May God bless you all! God bless America!

To Reporters after Meeting President Clinton
August 12

Mr. President,
Ladies and gentlemen,
I am pleased, Mr. President, that we have had this opportunity to talk together about some of the principal concerns of the world situation at this moment. The inalienable dignity of every human being and the rights which flow from that dignity—in the first place, the right to life and the defense of life—as well as the well-being and full human development of individuals and peoples, are at the heart of the themes on which the Church seeks a sincere and constructive dialogue with the leaders of the world's nations and representatives of the international community. I look forward to further contacts in the future, in the same spirit of mutual understanding and esteem which has always characterized relations between the United States and the Holy See.

I take this opportunity to thank you once more for welcoming me to the United States. I assure you that I pray each day for the leaders of government, that they may be wise and far-seeing servants of the common good and that their decisions and actions may bring genuine justice and peace to the world.

Thank you.

At Mile High Stadium
August 12

Dear young people,
Pilgrims on the path of life,
1. The Spirit of God has brought us to this eighth World Youth Day. On eight successive occasions young people from all parts of the world have heard the call of the Church and have traveled in order to be together—to be together with their bishops and the pope: fellow travelers on the path of life—in search of Christ. It is he, Jesus Christ, the true life, who gives hope and purpose to our earthly existence, opens our minds and hearts to the goodness and beauty of the world around us, to solidarity and friendship with our fellow human beings, to intimate communion with God himself, in a love that goes beyond all limits of time and space, to eternal, unassailable happiness.

This World Youth Day has brought us to Denver, a stupendous setting in the heart of the United States of America. I greet each one of you: "A great multitude which no man could number, from every nation, from all tribes and peoples and tongues" (Rev 7:9). I greet your bishops, your priests, your spiritual guides, your families. I thank you for being here. I thank everyone: Archbishop Stafford of Denver and his fellow workers; Archbishop Keeler, the president of the bishops' conference, and all the bishops; the bishops' commission for the organization of this World Youth Day; Cardinal Pironio and the Pontifical Council for the Laity; the civil authorities; the people of Denver and Colorado, who are our gracious hosts; the volunteers who are making sure that everything runs smoothly—I thank you all for your kindness, your hospitality and your good will.

Most of you are members of the Catholic Church; but others are from other Christian churches and communities, and I greet each one with sincere friendship. In spite of divisions among Christians, "all those justified by faith through baptism are incorporated into Christ... brothers and sisters in the Lord" (Unitatis redintegratio 3). Every meeting between young Catholics and other

> "If you want equal justice for all, and true freedom and lasting peace, then, America, defend life! All the great causes that are yours today will have meaning only to the extent that you guarantee the right to life and protect the human person."

young Christians must be one of discovering together ever more fully the riches of the Gospel message of life and love.

I greet all of you who have come from every corner of the United States, from every diocese of this vast country. Among you there is one group which I wish to mention with particular esteem: the Native American peoples. Thank you for bringing the richness and color of your special heritage to the World Youth Day. May Christ truly be the way, the truth and the life of your peoples!

Many are from the other two countries of North America:
—From Canada.
—(In Spanish) And so many from Mexico.
—Some of you are from the Caribbean.
—(In Spanish) Others from Central America. And from all the countries of South America.
—Many more are from Africa, Asia, Oceania and the Pacific, and so many from Europe.

2. At this point I wish to greet some of the groups present.

(In Spanish) An especially affectionate greeting to all the Spanish-speaking young people present: those from the United States, those from Latin America and from Spain. You are united, as heirs of a vibrant Catholic tradition, for which the Church is giving special thanks to God on the occasion of the fifth centenary of the evangelization of the Americas. May your generation be as constant and generous as past generations in making Jesus Christ known and loved.

(In French) To the French-speaking pilgrims, I hope that this journey of faith will strengthen your resolve to be ever more committed apostles to the world of youth. I greet those of you from France and from Canada. A special word of encouragement to the young people of Haitian origin, and I pray for the peace and harmony of your country.

(In Italian) To the young people from Italy: thanks for responding to the invitation to come to Denver in such large numbers. I am aware of the serious spiritual preparations you have made for this pilgrimage, and I am confident that you will reap benefits for your Christian life and witness.

(In German) I cordially greet the German-speaking young people who have come to express their faith in Jesus Christ, who came to give life in its fullness (cf. Jn 10:10). May these days of prayer and reflection, of meeting and joyful friendship with young people from all over the world, help you to be ever stronger and more confident in your service to the Church and to the world.

(In Portuguese) Dear friends from Portugal and from Brazil, Angola, Mozambique and Sao Tome and Principe. Jesus Christ is the hope of the world. May you discover his friendship and company ever more deeply during these days in Denver.

(In Polish) Praised be Jesus Christ! Young people from Poland, Denver is the continuation of Czestochowa. There we watched with the Black Madonna. Today, in Denver, we invoke her intercession on the Polish nation, especially on its young people, who must face the challenge of restoring truth and energy to society.... May Christ's promise of life, and life in abundance, come fully true in

your lives and in your works of apostolate and service.

(In Russian) Young people of the Russian language, be always open to the light of Christ, so that you can be his faithful witnesses.

(In Lithuanian) Young people from Lithuania: I am eagerly looking forward to my visit to your homeland in September. May the life and light of Christ illumine your hearts and give you courage! (In Croatian) Dear young people from Croatia, all of us gathered here for the World Youth Day are close to you in the very difficult situation of conflict which is causing so much suffering in the Balkans. May God inspire the leaders of the region and the international community to bring a speedy and just peace and thus avoid further casualties and destruction.

(In Arabic) The peace of Christ be with all the Arab-speaking young people who are here.

(In Tagalog) I cordially greet all the young people from the Philippines and of Philippine descent. May Christ always be the light of your lives and may he strengthen you for the challenges before you as witnesses to other young people.

(In Swahili) God bless you all with faith and hope and love.

(In Korean) May you be worthy heirs of St. Andrew Kim and his companion martyrs. They loved Christ to the end. May you too be his faithful disciples.

(In Vietnamese) Vietnamese young people, be strong and courageous in your Christian life.

3. (In English) We have come to Denver as pilgrims. We are continuing the journey made by millions of young people in the previous World Youth Days: to Rome, to Buenos Aires, to Santiago de Compostela, to Czestochowa.

Pilgrims set out for a destination. In our case it is not so much a place or a shrine that we seek to honor. Ours is a pilgrimage to a modern city, a symbolic destination: the "metropolis" is the place which determines the lifestyle and the history of a large part of the human family at the end of the twentieth century. This modern city of Denver is set in the beautiful natural surroundings of the Rocky Mountains, as if to put the work of human hands in relationship with the work of the Creator. We are therefore searching for the reflection of God not only in the beauty of nature but also in humanity's achievements and in each individual person. On this pilgrimage our steps are guided by the words of Jesus Christ: "I came that they may have life, and have it abundantly" (Jn 10:10).

My purpose in this first meeting with you is to invite you to enter into the depths of your hearts and to live the next few days as a real encounter with Jesus Christ.

Of course we are here to listen to one another: I to you, and you to the pope. But above all we are in Denver to hear the one true word of life—the eternal Word who was in the beginning with God; through whom all things were made, and without whom nothing was made that was made (cf. Jn 1:2-3). Young people of America and of the world, listen to what Christ the Redeemer is saying to you! "To all who received him, who believed in his name, he gave power to become children of God" (Jn 1:11-12). The World Youth

> "Young people of America and of the world, listen to what Christ the Redeemer is saying to you! 'To all who received him, who believed in his name, he gave power to become children of God.' The World Youth Day challenges you to be fully conscious of who you are as God's dearly beloved sons and daughters."

Day challenges you to be fully conscious of who you are as God's dearly beloved sons and daughters.

4. *(In Spanish)* Your pilgrimage through the city of Denver will lead you to meditate on Christ's promise of abundant life at different places along the way.

At St. Elizabeth's Church, the Holy Year cross will remind you where to look for the true life that Jesus gives. Jesus says: "Whoever does not take his cross and follow me is not worthy of me" (Mt 10:38). He says this, not because he does not love you enough, but because he is leading you to the discovery of authentic life and love. The life which Jesus gives can only be experienced through self-giving love, and self-giving love always implies some form of self-sacrifice: "Unless a grain of wheat falls into the earth and dies, it remains alone; but if it dies, it bears much fruit" (Jn 12:24). That is what the cross teaches.

(In French) At Holy Ghost Church your pilgrimage will lead you to Christ in the blessed Eucharist. In prayer before the Blessed Sacrament exposed you can pour out your hearts to him, but especially you must listen to what he has to say to each one of you. Christ's favorite words to young people are: "Fear not" (Mt 10:31) and "Come, follow me" (Mt 19:21). Who knows what the Lord will ask of you, young people of America, young men and women from Europe, Africa, Asia, Oceania?

(In Italian) At the Cathedral of the Immaculate Conception your pilgrimage will lead you to the icon of Our Lady of the New Advent. Mary, the Mother of the Redeemer, was her Son's first and best disciple. She will be present at every stage of our pilgrimage. She is the best guide we can have: she leads us to Christ and says: "Do whatever he tells you" (Jn 2:5).

(In English) Tomorrow, Friday, is meant to be a day of solidarity and penance. As a gesture of love toward our less fortunate brothers and sisters we are all asked to make a sacrifice at tomorrow's midday meal and to give what we save for St. Joseph's Hospital of Kitovu in Uganda, where many AIDS patients are being cared for with great love and attention. That region has been drastically affected by this dreaded disease and thousands of children have been left orphans as a result of it. Our gesture is a small sign of our love, an invitation to society not to neglect those who are suffering, especially when that suffering, which Jesus takes to himself (cf. Mt 25:36), can only be alleviated by the close, personal, caring presence of others.

Jesus has called each one of you to Denver for a purpose! You must live these days in such a way that, when the time comes to return home, each one of you will have a clearer idea of what Christ expects of you. Each one must have the courage to go and spread the good news among the people of the last part of the twentieth century, in particular among young people of your own age, who will take the Church and society into the next century.

And you, Latin-American youths, what does Christ ask of you? He is looking for collaborators in the new evangelization. He is looking for male and female missionaries of His Word to all peoples of this continent of hope. He is looking for builders of a new society, more just, more fraternal, more welcoming towards the "small ones" and the needy ones. Christ needs each one of you.

6. Lord Jesus Christ, send your Holy Spirit upon the young people who have set out to find you in the heart of the modern metropolis, especially during the catecheses of these days.

Be with us all at the great gathering of the pilgrims on the path of life, when at the vigil of the feast of Mary's Assumption into heaven and at the Mass on that day, the young people of the United States, of the Americas, of the world, will proclaim and celebrate their faith in you, you who alone have the words which unlock the depths of the mystery of true life.

O Mary, Our Lady of the New Advent, who kept all these things, pondering them in your heart (cf. Lk 2:19), teach these young people to be good listeners to your Son, the Word of life.

Pray for them that no barriers will stand in the way of their discovering the new life which your Son brought into the world.

Virgin daughter of Sion, guide each step of our way along the path that leads to life!

Young people of the eighth World Youth Day, rise to the challenge which Denver sets before you:

Follow the "pilgrim" cross.

Go in search of God, because he can also be found in the heart of a modern city.

Recognize him in so many young people full of hope and noble ideals.

Feel the breath of the Holy Spirit among so many different races and cultures, all united in acknowledging Christ as the way, the truth and the life of every human being (cf. Angelus, April 5, 1993).

Dear young friends, in the name of Jesus Christ I greet you and bless you!

With great joy I look forward to our next meeting.

Hasta la vista!

To the United States Bishops in the Denver Cathedral
August 13

"On this rock I will build my church" (Mt 16:18).

Dear brother bishops,
1. These words of Christ, which he pronounced near Caesarea Philippi, resound again today in the cathedral of Denver. Here, in Colorado, at the foot of the Rocky Mountains, they acquire a special significance. What is this rock on which Christ builds his Church? Rather, who is this rock? This is the order of the questions which Christ's words suggest.

Illumined by the grace of revelation, Simon says who Jesus is: "You are the Christ, the son of the living God" (Mt 16:16). The Father himself communicates the truth about Jesus to Peter, in whom this truth comes alive through his obedience of faith (cf. Rom 16:26). "Blest are you, Simon, son of John! No mere man has revealed this to you, but my heavenly Father" (Mt 16:17). First, Peter receives the inner revelation of truth in his heart, then he confesses this truth on his lips.

Replying, Jesus says who Simon is—"You are Peter" (Mt 16:18); that is, you are Rock. It is the person of Peter, insofar as he confesses the apostolic faith, who is the living stone, assimilated to Christ as the Church's foundation (cf. Eph 2:20).

This is the rock on which Christ built his Church from the beginning.

2. From the altar of the cathedral of Denver I warmly greet each one of you who are taking part in the World Youth Day. You are here, just as I am, out of fidelity to our specific ministry in the Church. We are here to be with the young pilgrims, during these days in which we are witnesses of the grace of the Holy Spirit at work in so many generous young hearts.

In a sense we, the pastors, have been called here by the young people themselves. Their response to the World Youth Day clearly indicates that they have perceived something of what the eternal Father reveals to the "little ones" (cf. Mt 11:25). They are thirsty to know more, to penetrate more deeply into the mystery of Christ and the Church. They know that the Father can open that door to them, just as he revealed the heart of the mystery to Peter at Caesarea Philippi.

In this interior advancement of grace, we bishops and priests have a great responsibility. Are we always ready to help young people discover the transcendent elements of the Christian life? From our words and actions do they conclude that the Church is indeed a mystery of communion with the Blessed Trinity, and not just a human institution with temporal aims? Through our ministry the young people present here need to be able to discover, above all, that they are temples of God and that the Spirit of God dwells in them (cf. 1 Cor 3:16).

These are the days in which the light of the Gospel must shine before them with a particular brilliance.

For they are the Church of today and tomorrow—the Church that rises on the rock of divine truth, on the rock of the apostolic faith. The Church of the third millennium needs to be firmly planted in the heart of the new generation of the sons and daughters of the living God.

3. Venerable and dear brothers!

Let us commend these days to Mary, the seat of wisdom. Let us entrust to her all the young people who have come here. Let us entrust to her the Church of the young throughout the world, in every country and on every continent.

Let us entrust to her prayers ourselves and our brother priests, all those who live the consecrated life, all our brothers and sisters in the faith. May she guide our ministry here in Denver. And may this whole experience of the World Youth Day be for us a reawakening of trust in the "keys of the kingdom of heaven," which Christ entrusted to the Church in the person of Peter (cf. Mt 16:19). Amen.

At the Way of the Cross, Mile High Stadium
August 13

"Behold, the Lamb of God, who takes away the sins of the world" (cf. Jn 1:29).

1. Accused before a judge who condemns more out of fear and cynicism than out of conviction, Jesus is a victim of human pride and corrupt justice. Tortured and mocked, he is the image of what human beings are capable of doing to others when their hearts are hardened and the light of conscience is dimmed. But, in the eyes of the Father, Jesus is the beloved Son, the innocent lamb who goes to the slaughter for our sins: "Upon him was the chastisement that makes us whole, by his stripes we were healed" (Is 53:5).

From his self-sacrifice spring forgiveness and reconciliation for all. Even on the Cross Jesus had words of love: "Father, forgive them; they do not know what they are doing" (Lk 23:34). That love reaches out to everyone without exception. The Gospel of St. John records the prophetic words: "They will look upon him whom they have pierced" (Jn 19:37). From his side, pierced by the soldier's lance, flow blood and water (cf. Jn 19:34), the sign of the life-giving grace that fills the Church with new life, the new life that reaches us through the sacraments.

2. Young people of the World Youth Day, in this Way of the Cross you have looked upon the face of the suffering Christ, and adored the Lord raised up between earth and heaven. Before this terrible injustice and these terrible sufferings, only the words which God spoke through the prophet Isaiah can turn our anguished sadness into hope:

"See, my servant shall prosper,
"He shall be raised high and greatly exalted....
"Through his suffering, my servant shall justify many,
"And their guilt he shall bear....
"He shall take away the sins of many
"And win pardon for their offenses" (Is 52:13, 53:11-12). Young people, you are a special part of Christ's inheritance, the people won by the love of the Redeemer.

Take courage in the face of life's difficulties and injustices. Commit yourselves to the struggle for justice, solidarity and peace in the world. Offer your youthful energies and your talents to building a civilization of Christian love. Be witnesses of God's love for the innocent and the weak, for the poor and the oppressed.

3. The Way of the Cross has led you to the heart of the mystery of God's redeeming love, the mystery which is at the center of the Church's life, the mystery which is the core of all Christian witness and teaching. There is much to think and pray about. The World Youth Day has reached a moment of particular intensity. Here, the example of Mary can show us the way forward: "Mary kept all these things, reflecting on them in her heart" (Lk 2:19).

I invite you to create a climate of silence and reflection, so that a deepening awareness of the mystery can grow in every young person gathered here. Let us pray that the love which God pours into our hearts through the Holy Spirit (cf. Rom 5:5) may not be blocked or hindered by passing distractions.

In that silence, may inner peace come to you, a peace which can be deepened and more fully possessed through the sacrament of reconciliation—"in Christ God was reconciling the world to himself, not counting our trespasses against us, and entrusting to us the message of reconciliation.... I beseech you on behalf of Christ, be reconciled to God" (cf. 2 Cor 5:19-20).

I hope that you will avail yourselves of the many priests who are here. In the sacrament of penance they are ambassadors to you of Christ's loving forgiveness.

> "From his self-sacrifice spring forgiveness and reconciliation for all. Even on the Cross Jesus had words of love: 'Father, forgive them; they do not know what they are doing.'"

4. On the first day of the week, at dawn, the women came to the tomb. They found the stone rolled back and a messenger who said:

"Why do you search for the Living One among the dead? He is not here; he has been raised up. Remember what he said to you while he was still in Galilee—that the Son of Man must be delivered unto the hands of sinful men, and be crucified, and on the third day rise again" (Lk 24:5-7).

The new life that has burst forth in the Resurrection is the world's only hope.

In the name of Christ, in the name of the Church, in the name of needy humanity: I encourage you to have that new life in you! Be witnesses of that new life to the world around you.

Youth Forum Mass at The Cathedral
August 14

"Go into all the world" (Mk 16:15).

1. The final words of Christ to his apostles in St. Mark's Gospel are these: "Go into all the world and preach the Gospel to the whole creation." This is the missionary mandate. This is the command which began the great expansion of the Church from the first group of disciples in Jerusalem to the great Christian family spread throughout the world. The Church lives among every people and nation: as is clearly demonstrated here by your presence, young representatives to the International Youth Forum, from almost every country in the world.

Christ addressed those challenging words to the apostles; the same ones to whom he had already said, some time before: "Follow me" (Mk 1:17). He had said: "Follow me" to each one, individually, in a personal way. And between that initial calling and the final sending "into all the world," each one of those disciples underwent an experience, a process of growth, which prepared them intimately for the enormous challenge and adventure which was Christ's parting summons to them.

Christ first invites, then he reveals himself more fully, and then he sends. He invites in order to make himself known to those whom he wishes to send. He sends those who have come to know the mystery of his person and of his Kingdom. For the Gospel must be proclaimed through the power of their witness. And the strength of their witness depends on knowledge and love of Jesus Christ himself. Every apostle must be able to identify with what the First Letter of John says:

"This is what we proclaim to you:
"What was from the beginning,
"What we have heard,
"What we have seen with our eyes,
"What we have looked upon
"And our hands have touched—
"We speak of the word of life" (1 Jn 1:1).

2. That same Gospel experience penetrates the whole World Youth Day. The young people who are gathering here from all parts of the world, and you in particular, participants in the International Youth Forum, are involved in a similar process: at some point Christ entered your lives and invited you to a greater awareness of your baptismal consecration; with God's grace and the help of a believing community you grew in understanding of your Christian identity and your role in the Church and in society. As mature Catholics, you began to take an active part in the apostolate.

Denver is the sum of countless experiences of this kind. In your families, parishes, schools, Catholic associations and movements, the seed of a genuine faith was planted and grew until you heard in your own hearts the echo of those original words: "Come, follow me" (Lk 18:22). Each one of you has followed a different path, but you have not been alone on this journey. At every stage the Church has assisted and encouraged you, through her ministers, her religious, and so many active members of the laity. The path finally led to the International Youth Forum. And now, here in Denver, the challenge before you is to recognize the full implications of the Lord's words: "Go into the whole world and proclaim the good news" (Mk 16:15).

Yes, Christ the Lord is the very heart of the World Youth Day, and he continues to invite many young people to join him in the sublime task of spreading his Kingdom. He is here because the Church is here. He is here in the Eucharist, and through the ministry of his priests and bishops, in union with the successor of Peter. Christ is here through the faith and love of so many young people who have prepared themselves spiritually for this meeting and have worked hard and made sacrifices in order to be able to make this pilgrimage of hope and commitment.

3. In a sense, the International Youth Forum represents the nucleus of the World Youth Day. Not only are you praying and reflecting on the theme of the life in abundance which Christ came to give (cf. Jn 10:10), but you are comparing experiences of the apostolate in different parts of the world, in order to learn from one another and to be confirmed in the Christian leadership which you are called to exercise among your contemporaries. Only a great love of Christ and of the Church will sustain you in the apostolate awaiting you when you return home.

As leaders in the field of the youth apostolate, your task will be to help your parishes, dioceses, associations and movements to be truly open to the personal, social and spiritual needs of young people. You will have to find ways of involving young people in projects and activities of formation, spirituality and service, giving them responsibility for themselves and their work and taking care to avoid isolating them and their apostolate from the rest of the ecclesial community. Young people need to be able to see the practical relevance of their efforts to meet the real needs of people, especially the poor and neglected. They should also be able to see that their apostolate belongs fully to the Church's mission in the world.

Have no fear! Denver, like the previous World Youth Days, is a time of grace: a great gathering of young people, all speaking different languages but all united in proclaiming the mystery of Christ and of the new life he gives. This is especially evident in the catecheses being given each day in various languages. In prayer and song, so many different tongues ring out in praise of God. All this makes Denver a reflection of what happened in Jerusalem at Pentecost (cf. Acts 2:1-4). Out of all the diversity of the young people gathered here—diversity of origin, race and language—the Spirit of truth will create the deep and abiding unity of commitment to the new evangelization, in which the defense of human life, the promotion of human rights and the fostering of a civilization of love are urgent tasks.

4. To be committed to the new evangelization means that we are convinced that we have something of value to offer to the human family at the dawn of the new millennium. All of us who have come here—young people and their pastors, bishops and the pope—must be aware that it is not enough to offer a "merely human wisdom, a pseudo-science of well-being" (Redemptoris Missio 11). We must be convinced that we have "a pearl of great price" (cf. Mt 13:46), a great "treasure" (cf. Mt 13:44), which is fundamental to the earthly existence and eternal salvation of every member of the human race.

The call of the prophet Isaiah, narrated in the first reading of this Mass, can begin to unveil the mystery to us. Whenever God communicates with a human being, the essence of that communication is a revelation of his own holiness: "My eyes have seen the King, the Lord of hosts.... Holy, holy, holy is the Lord of hosts!" (Is 6:5, 3). And our response can be none other than joyous openness to that divine glory and acceptance of its implications for the meaning and purpose of our lives.

The ineffable experience of God's holiness lives on in the Church. Every day in the very center of the eucharistic liturgy we repeat the words: "Holy, holy, holy Lord, God of power and might. Heaven and earth are full of your glory" (cf. Is 6:3).

This treasure lives on in the Church because the holiness of God is revealed in all its fullness through Jesus Christ: "For God who said, 'Let light shine out of darkness,' has shone in our hearts, that we in turn might make known the glory of God shining on the face of Christ" (2 Cor 4:6).

The holiness of God shines forth in Christ, the Emmanuel, God with us. Behold, "the Word became flesh and dwelt among us, and we have seen his glory, the glory of the only Son coming from the Father" (Jn 1:14)—and we have seen him, heard him and touched him: at the Lake of Galilee, on the Mount of the Beatitudes, on Mount Tabor, on Golgotha, along the road to Emmaus, in the Eucharist, in prayer, in the tangible experience of every vocation, especially when the Lord calls certain individuals to follow him more closely along the path of religious consecration or priestly ministry. We know that Christ never abandons his Church. At a time like this, when many are confused regarding the fundamental truths and values on which to build their lives and seek their eternal salvation, when many Catholics are in danger of losing their faith—the pearl of great price—when there are not enough priests, not enough religious sisters and brothers to give support and guidance, not enough contemplative religious to keep before people's eyes the sense of the absolute supremacy of God, we must be convinced that Christ is knocking at many hearts, looking for young people like you to send into the vineyard, where an abundant harvest is ready.

5. "But we—we human beings—have this treasure in earthen vessels" (cf. 2 Cor 4:7). That is why we are often afraid of the demands of the Redeemer's love. We may try to appease our conscience by giving of ourselves, but in limited and partial ways, or in ways that we like—not always in the ways that the Lord suggests. Yet, the fact that we carry this treasure in earthen vessels serves to make it clear that "its surpassing power comes from God and not from us" (2 Cor 4:7). Wherever young men and women allow the grace of Christ to work in them and produce new life, the extraordinary power of divine love is released into their lives and into the life of the community. It transforms their attitude and behavior and inevitably attracts others to follow the same adventurous path. This power comes from God and not from us.

The one who has invited you to Denver, and who can call you at any stage of your pilgrimage through life, wants you to have the treasure of knowing him more fully. He wants to occupy the central place in your hearts, and therefore he purifies your love and tests your courage. The realization of his hidden but certain presence acts like a burning coal that touches your lips (cf. Is 6:7) and makes you able to repeat the eternal Yes of the Son, as the Letter to the Hebrews says: "Then I said, `As it is written of me in the book, I have come to do your will, O God'" (Heb 10:7). That Yes guided every step of the Son of Man: "Jesus said to them, `Truly, truly, I say to you, the Son can do nothing of his own accord, but only what he sees the Father doing'" (Jn 5:19). And Mary gave the very same Yes to God's plan for her life: "Let it be done to me as you say" (Lk 1:38).

6. Christ is asking the young people of the World Youth Day: "Whom shall I send?" (Is 6:8).

And, with fervor, let each one respond: "Here am I! Send me" (Is 6:8).

Do not forget the needs of your homelands! Heed the cry of the poor and the oppressed in the countries and continents from which you come! Be convinced that the Gospel is the only path of genuine liberation and salvation for the world's peoples: "Your salvation, O Lord, is for all the peoples" (Responsorial Psalm, Ps 95).

Everyone who, in response to Christ's invitation, comes to Denver to take part in the World Youth Day must hear his words: "Go... and proclaim the good news" (Mk 16:15).

Let us earnestly pray the Lord of the harvest that the youth of the world will not hesitate to reply: "Here am I! Send me!" "Send us!" Amen.

At the Prayer Service in McNichols Arena
August 14

"The mountain of the Lord's house shall be established as the highest mountain" (Is 2:2).

Dear brothers and sisters in Christ,
1. Upon arriving in Denver I lifted up my eyes toward the splendor of the Rocky Mountains, whose majesty and power recall that all our help comes from the Lord who has made heaven and earth (cf. Ps 121:1). He alone is the rock of our salvation (cf. Ps 89:26). God has given me the grace to join my voice with yours in praising and thanking our heavenly Father for the "mighty works" (Acts 2:12) that he has accomplished since the Gospel was first preached in this region.

Today I greet all those whom Christ—the "pescador de hombres," the divine Fisherman—has gathered into the net of his Church. "With the affection of Christ Jesus" (Phil 1:8), I thank Archbishop Stafford of Denver, Bishop Hanifen of Colorado Springs, Bishop Tafoya of Pueblo, Bishop Hart of Cheyenne and the other bishops present: the priests, the religious and every one of you, for being "sound in faith, in love, and in steadfastness" (Titus 2:2).

I cordially greet the governor of Colorado, the mayor of Denver and the representatives of other churches, ecclesial communities and religious bodies. Your presence encourages us to continue to strive for ever-greater understanding among all people of good will and to work together for a new civilization of love.

2. The World Youth Day is a great celebration of life: life as a divine gift and an awe-inspiring mystery. Young people from all over the world are gathering to profess the Church's faith that in Jesus Christ we can come to the full truth about our human condition and our eternal destiny.

Only in Christ can men and women find answers to the ultimate questions that trouble them. Only in Christ can they fully understand their dignity as persons created and loved by God. Jesus Christ is "the only Son from the Father... full of grace and truth" (Jn 1:14).

By keeping the incarnation of the eternal Word before her eyes, the Church understands more fully her twofold nature—human and divine. She is the mystical body of the Word made flesh. As such she is inseparably united with her Lord and is holy in a way that can never fail (cf. Lumen gentium 39). The Church is also the visible means which God uses to reconcile sinful humanity to himself. She is the people of God making its pilgrim way to the Father's house. In this sense she is constantly in need of conversion and renewal, and her members must ever be challenged "to purify and renew themselves so that the sign of Christ can shine more brightly on (her) face" (Lumen gentium 15). Only when the Church generates works of genuine holiness and humble service do the words of Isaiah come true: "All nations shall stream toward her" (Is 2:2).

United to Christ as a visible communion of persons, the Church must take as her model the early Christian community in Jerusalem which devoted itself "to the apostles' teaching and fellowship, to the breaking of bread and the prayers" (Acts 2:42). If the Church is to be a credible sign of reconciliation to the world, all those who believe, wherever they may be, must be "of one heart and one soul" (Acts 4:32). By your fraternal communion the world will know that you are Christ's disciples!

3. The members of the Catholic Church should take to heart the plea of St. Paul: always be "eager to maintain the unity of the Spirit in the bond of peace" (Eph 4:3). With gentleness and patience, revere the Church as Christ's beloved bride who is ever vigorous and youthful. So many problems arise when people think of the Church as "theirs," when in fact she belongs to Christ. Christ and the Church are inseparably united as "one flesh" (cf. Eph 5:29). Our love for Christ finds its vital expression in our love for the Church. Polarization and destructive criticism have no place among "those who are of the household of faith" (Gal 6:10). The Church in the United States is vital and dynamic, rich in "faith and love and holiness" (1 Tim 2:15). By far the vast majority of her bishops, priests, religious and laity are dedicated followers of Christ and generous servants of the Gospel message of love. Nevertheless, at a time when all institutions are suspect, the Church herself has not escaped reproach. I have already written to the bishops of the United States about the pain of the suffering and scandal caused by the sins of some ministers of the altar. Sad situations such as these invite us anew to look at the mystery of the Church with the eyes of faith. While every human means for

> "Only in Christ can men and women find answers to the ultimate questions that trouble them. Only in Christ can they fully understand their dignity as persons created and loved by God. Jesus Christ is 'the only Son from the Father... full of grace and truth.'"

responding to this evil must be implemented, we cannot forget that the first and most important means is prayer: ardent, humble, confident prayer. America needs much prayer—lest it lose its soul (cf. Letter to the bishops of the United States, June 11, 1993).

4. On many issues, especially with regard to moral questions, "the teaching of the Church in our day is placed in a social and cultural context which renders it more difficult to understand and yet more urgent and irreplaceable for promoting the true good of men and women" (Familiaris consortio 30). Nowhere is this more evident than in questions relating to the transmission of human life and to the inalienable right to life of the unborn.

Twenty-five years ago Pope Paul VI published the encyclical Humanae vitae. Your bishops recently issued a statement to mark this anniversary. They call everyone "to listen to the wisdom of Humanae vitae and to make the Church's teaching the foundation for a renewed understanding of marriage and family life" (NCCB, "Human Sexuality from God's Perspective: 'Humanae Vitae' 25 Years Later," conclusion). The Church calls married couples to responsible parenthood by acting as "ministers"—and not "arbiters"—of God's saving plan. Since the publication of Humanae vitae, significant steps have been taken to promote natural family planning among those who wish to live their conjugal love according to the fullness of its truth. Yet more efforts must be made to educate the consciences of married couples in this form of conjugal chastity, which is grounded on "dialogue, reciprocal respect, shared responsibility and self-control" (Familiaris consortio, 32). I appeal especially to young people to rediscover the wealth of wisdom, the integrity of conscience and the deep interior joy which flow from respect for human sexuality understood as a great gift from God and lived according to the truth of the body's nuptial meaning.

5. Likewise, building an authentic civilization of love must include a massive effort to educate consciences in the moral truths which sustain respect for life in the face of every threat against it. In her vigorous concern for human rights and justice, the Catholic Church is unambiguously committed to protecting and cherishing every human life, including the life of the unborn. As sent by Christ to serve the weak, downtrodden and defenseless, the Church must speak on behalf of those most in need of protection. It is a source of comfort that this position is shared by people of many faiths. Those who respect life must accompany their teaching about the value of every human life with concrete and effective acts of solidarity to people in difficult situations. Without charity, the struggle to defend life would be lacking the essential ingredient of the Christian ethic; as St. Paul writes: "Do not be overcome by evil, but overcome evil with good" (Rom 12:21).

Archbishop Stafford has told me of the deep concern of many Americans about urban violence as a negative "sign of the times" that needs to be read in light of the Gospel. Violence is always a failure to respect God's image and likeness (cf. Gen 1:26-27) in our neighbor, in every human person, without exception. Violence in any form is a denial of human dignity. The question which must be asked is: Who is responsible? Individuals have a responsibility for what is happening. Families have a responsibility. Society has a heavy responsibility. Everybody must be willing to accept their part of this responsibility, including the media which in part seem to be becoming more aware of the effect they can have on their audiences.

And when the question is asked: What is to be done? Everybody must be committed to fostering a profound sense of the value of life and dignity of the human person. The whole of society must work to change the structural conditions which lead people, especially the young, to the lack of vision, the loss of esteem for themselves and for others which lead to violence. But since the root of violence is in the human heart, society will be condemned to go on causing it, feeding it, and even, to an extent, glorifying it, unless it reaffirms the moral and religious truths which alone are an effective barrier to lawlessness and violence, because these truths alone are capable of enlightening and strengthening conscience. Ultimately, it is the victory of grace over sin that leads to fraternal harmony and reconciliation.

6. Brothers and sisters in Christ, I urge you to renew your trust in the richness of the Father's mercy (cf. Eph 2:4), in the incarnation and redemption accomplished by his beloved Son, in the Holy Spirit's vivifying presence in your hearts. This immense mystery of love is made present to us through holy Church's sacraments, teaching and solidarity with pilgrim humanity. The Church, through your bishops and other ministers, in your parishes, associations and movements, needs your love and your active support in defending the inviolable right to life and the integrity of the family, in promoting Christian principles in private and public life, in serving the poor and the weak, and in overcoming all manner of evil with good.

May Mary, "full of grace," intercede for the Catholic community of Colorado and of the United States. May her example of discipleship draw each one of you to an ever more personal love of her Son our Lord Jesus Christ. May she who is the Mother of the Church teach you to love and serve the Church as she loved and served the first community of Christ's followers (cf. Acts 1:14). Through the Church, may you abide in Christ, the Prince of peace and the Lord of our lives. Amen.

At the Prayer Vigil with Youth, Cherry Creek State Park

August 14

FIRST PART

Dear young people,
Young pilgrims on the path of life:

"I came that they might have life, and have it abundantly" (Jn 10:10).

1. This evening these words of Christ are addressed to you, young people gathered for the World Youth Day.

Jesus speaks these words in the parable of the Good Shepherd. The Good Shepherd: what a beautiful image of God! It transmits something deep and personal about the way God cares for all that he has made. In the modern metropolis it is not likely that you will see a shepherd guarding his flock. But we can go back to the traditions of the Old Testament, in which the parable is deeply rooted, in

order to understand the loving care of the shepherd for his sheep.

The psalm says: "The Lord is my shepherd, I shall not want" (Ps 23:1). The Lord, the shepherd, is God-Yahweh. The one who freed his people from oppression in the land of their exile. The one who revealed himself on Mount Sinai as the God of the covenant: "If you will obey my voice and keep my covenant, you shall be my own possession among all peoples; for all the earth is mine" (Ex 19:5).

God is the creator of all that exists. On the earth which he created he placed man and woman: "male and female he created them" (Gen 1:27). "And God blessed them, and God said to them, 'Be fruitful and multiply, and fill the earth and subdue it; and have dominion over… every living thing that moves upon the earth'" (Gen 1:28).

2. The special place of human beings in all that God made lies in their being given a share in God's own concern and providence for the whole of creation. The Creator has entrusted the world to us, as a gift and as a responsibility. He who is Eternal Providence, the one who guides the entire universe toward its final destiny, made us in his image and likeness, so that we, too, should become "providence"—a wise and intelligent providence, guiding human development and the development of the world along the path of harmony with the Creator's will, for the well-being of the human family and the fulfillment of each individual's transcendent calling.

3. (In Spanish) Yet, millions of men and women live without making sense out of what they do and what happens to them. Here this evening, in Cherry Creek State Park in Denver, you represent the youth of the world, with all the questions which the young people at the end of the twentieth century have a need and a right to ask.

Our theme is life, and life is full of mystery. Science and technology have made enormous progress in uncovering the secrets of our natural life, but even a superficial examination of our personal experience shows that there are many other dimensions to our individual and collective existence on this planet. Our restless hearts reach out beyond our own limits, on the wings of our capacity to think and love: to think and love the immeasurable, the infinite, the absolute and supreme form of being. Our interior gaze extends to the limitless horizons of our hopes and aspirations. And in the midst of all of life's contradictions, we search for life's true meaning. We wonder and ask, Why?

Why am I here?
Why am I alive at all?
What must I do?

None of you is alone in posing these questions. Humanity as a whole feels the pressing need to give sense and purpose to a world which is increasingly complicated and difficult to be happy in. The bishops of the world gathered at the Second Vatican Council expressed it this way: "In the face of the modern development of the world, an ever-increasing number of people are raising the most basic questions.…What is man? What is the sense of sorrow, of evil, of death, which continues to exist despite so much progress?… What can man offer to society? What can he expect from it? What follows this earthly life?" (Gaudium et spes 10).

To fail to ask these basic questions is to miss the great adventure of the search for the truth about life.

4. (In English) You know how easy it is to avoid the fundamental questions. But your presence here shows that you will not hide from reality and from responsibility!

You care about the gift of life that God has given you. You have confidence in Christ when he says: "I came that they may have life, and have it abundantly" (Jn 10:10).

Our vigil begins with an act of trust in the words of the Good Shepherd. In Jesus Christ, the Father expresses the whole truth concerning creation. We believe that in the life, death and Resurrection of Jesus the Father reveals all his love for humanity. That is why Christ calls himself "the sheepgate" (Jn 10:7). As the gate, he stands guard over the creatures entrusted to him. He leads them to the good pastures: "I am the gate. Whoever enters through me will be safe. He will go in and out, and find pasture" (Jn 10:9).

Jesus Christ is truly the world's shepherd. Our hearts must be open to his words. For this we have come to this world meeting of youth: from every state and diocese in the United States, from all over the Americas, from every continent: all represented here by the flags which your delegates have set up to show that no one here this evening is a stranger. We are all one in Christ. The Lord has led us as he leads the flock:

The Lord is our shepherd; we shall not want.
In green pastures he makes us find rest.
Beside restful waters he leads us;
He refreshes our souls.
Even though we walk in a dark valley
we fear no evil; for he is at our side.
He gives us courage (cf. Ps 23).

As we reflect together on the life which Jesus gives, I ask you to have the courage to commit yourselves to the truth. Have the courage to believe the good news about life which Jesus teaches in the Gospel. Open your minds and hearts to the beauty of all that God has made and to his special, personal love for each one of you.

Young people of the world, hear his voice!
Hear his voice and follow him!
Only the Good Shepherd will lead you to the full truth about life.

SECOND PART

I

1. At this point the young people gathered in Denver may ask: What is the pope going to say about life?

My words will be a profession of the faith of Peter, the first pope. My message can be none other than what has been handed on from the beginning, because it is not mine but the good news of Jesus Christ himself.

The New Testament presents Simon—whom Jesus called Peter, the Rock—as a vigorous, passionate disciple of Christ. But he also doubted and, at a decisive moment, he even denied that he was a follower of Jesus. Yet, despite these human weaknesses, Peter was the first disciple to make a full public profession of faith in the Master. One day Jesus asked: "Who do you say that I am?" And Peter answered: "You are the Christ, the son of the living God" (Mt 16:16).

Beginning with Peter, the first apostolic witness, multitudes of witnesses, men and women, young and old, of every nation on earth, have proclaimed their faith in Jesus Christ, true God and true man, the Redeemer of man, the Lord of history, the Prince of peace. Like Peter, they asked: "To whom shall we go? You have the words

of eternal life" (Jn 6:68).

This evening we profess the same faith as Peter. We believe that Jesus Christ has the words of life, and that he speaks those words to the Church, to all who open their minds and hearts to him with faith and trust.

2. "I am the Good Shepherd. The Good Shepherd lays down his life for the sheep" (Jn 10:11). Our first reflection is inspired by these words of Jesus in the Gospel of St. John.

The Good Shepherd lays down his life. Death assails life.

At the level of our human experience, death is the enemy of life. It is an intruder who frustrates our natural desire to live. This is especially obvious in the case of untimely or violent death, and most of all in the case of the killing of the innocent. It is not surprising then that among the Ten Commandments the Lord of life, the God of the covenant, should have said on Mount Sinai, "You shall not kill" (Ex 20:13; cf. Mt 5:21).

The words "You shall not kill" were engraved on the tablets of the covenant—on the stone tablets of the law. But, even before that, this law was engraved on the human heart, in the sanctuary of every individual's conscience. In the Bible, the first to experience the force of this law was Cain, who murdered his brother Abel. Immediately after his terrible crime, he felt the whole weight of having broken the commandment not to kill. Even though he tried to escape from the truth, saying: "Am I my brother's keeper?" (Gen 4:9), the inner voice repeated over and over: "You are a murderer." The voice was his conscience, and it could not be silenced.

3. (In French) With the passing of time the threats to life do not lessen. They grow enormous. Not just threats from outside, from the forces of nature or from some "Cain" who murders "Abel"—but threats programmed in a scientific and systematic way. The twentieth century has been a time of massive attacks against life, an unending series of wars and a continuing slaughter of innocent human beings. The false prophets and the false teachers have been very successful.

Likewise, false models of progress have led to endangering the earth's proper ecological balance. Man—made in the image and likeness of the Creator—was meant to be the Good Shepherd of the environment in which he exists and lives. This is an ancient task, which the human family carried out with fair success down through history, until in recent times man himself has become the destroyer of his own natural environment. In some places this has already happened or is happening.

But not only that. There is spreading, too, an anti-life mentality—an attitude of hostility to life in the womb and life in its last stages. Precisely when science and medicine are achieving a greater capacity to safeguard health and life, the threats against life are becoming more insidious. Abortion and euthanasia—the actual killing of another human being—are hailed as "rights" and solutions to "problems"—an individual's problem or society's. The slaughter of the innocents is no less sinful and devastating simply because it is done in a legal and scientific way. In the modern metropolis, life—God's first gift, and the fundamental right of every individual, on which all other rights are based—is often treated as just one

> "My words will be a profession of the faith of Peter, the first pope. My message can be none other than what has been handed on from the beginning, because it is not mine but the good news of Jesus Christ himself."

more commodity to be organized, commercialized and manipulated according to convenience. *(In Italian)* All this happens while Christ, the Good Shepherd, wants us to "have life." He sees everything that threatens life. He sees the wolf coming to ravage and scatter the sheep. He sees all those who try to get in to the sheepfold but who are thieves and robbers (cf. Jn 10:1-13). He sees so many young people throwing away their lives in a flight into irresponsibility and falsehood. Drug and alcohol abuse, pornography and sexual disorder, violence: These are grave social problems which call for a serious response from the whole of society, within each country and on the international level. But they are also personal tragedies, and they need to be met with concrete interpersonal acts of love and solidarity, in a great rebirth of the sense of personal answerability before God, before others and before our own conscience. We are our brothers' keepers! (cf. Gen 4:9).

II

4. *(In English)* Why do the consciences of young people not rebel against this situation, especially against the moral evil which flows from personal choices? Why do so many acquiesce in attitudes and behavior which offend human dignity and disfigure the image of God in us? The normal thing would be for conscience to point out the mortal danger to the individual and to humanity contained in the easy acceptance of evil and sin. And yet, it is not always so. Is it because conscience itself is losing the ability to distinguish good from evil?

In a technological culture in which people are used to dominating matter, discovering its laws and mechanisms in order to transform it according to their wishes, the danger arises of also wanting to manipulate conscience and its demands. In a culture which holds that no universally valid truths are possible, nothing is absolute. Therefore, in the end—they say—objective goodness and evil no longer really matter. Good comes to mean what is pleasing or useful at a particular moment. Evil means what contradicts our subjective wishes. Each person can build a private system of values.

5. Young people, do not give in to this widespread false morality. Do not stifle your conscience! Conscience is the most secret core and sanctuary of a person, where we are alone with God (cf. Gaudium et spes 16). "In the depths of his conscience man detects a law which he does not impose upon himself, but which holds him to obedience" (Gaudium et spes 16). That law is not an external human law but the voice of God, calling us to free ourselves from the grip of evil desires and sin and stimulating us to seek what is good and true. Only by listening to the voice of God in your most intimate being and by acting in accordance with its directions will you reach the freedom you yearn for. As Jesus said, only the truth will make you free (cf. Jn 8:32). And the truth is not the fruit of each individual's imagination. God gave you intelligence to know the truth and your will to achieve what is morally good. He has given you the light of conscience to guide your moral decisions, to love good and avoid evil. Moral truth is objective, and a properly formed conscience can perceive it.

But if conscience itself has been corrupted, how can it be restored? If conscience—which is light—no longer enlightens, how can we overcome the moral darkness? Jesus says: "The eye is the body's lamp. If your eyes are good, your body will be filled with light; if your eyes are bad, your body will be in darkness. And if your light is darkness, how deep will the darkness be!" (Mt 6:22-23).

But Jesus also says: "I am the light of the world. No follower of mine shall ever walk in darkness; no, he shall possess the light of life" (Jn 8:12). If you follow Christ, you will restore conscience to its rightful place and proper role, and you will be the light of the world, the salt of the earth (cf. Mt 5:13).

A rebirth of conscience must come from two sources: first, the effort to know objective truth with certainty, including the truth about God; and secondly, the light of faith in Jesus Christ, who alone has the words of life.

6. *(In Spanish)* Against the splendid backdrop of the Colorado mountains, with their pure air which bestows peace and serenity on nature, the soul rises spontaneously to sing the praise of the Creator: "O Lord, our Lord, how glorious is your name over all the earth!" (Ps 8:2).

Young pilgrims, the visible world is like a map which points to heaven, the eternal dwelling place of the living God. We learn to see the Creator by contemplating the beauty of his creatures. In this world, the goodness, wisdom and almighty power of God shine forth. And human intelligence, even after original sin—provided it is not clouded by error or passion—can discover the hand of the artist in the wonderful works he has made. Reason can know God through the book of nature: a personal, infinitely good, wise, powerful, eternal God, who transcends the world and at the same time is present in the innermost being of his creatures. St. Paul writes: "Since the creation of the world, invisible realities, God's eternal power and divinity, have become visible, recognized through the things he has made" (Rom 1:20).

Jesus taught us to see the hand of the Father in the beauty of the lilies of the field, the birds of the air, the night sky, the fields ready for the harvest, in the faces of children, in the needs of the poor and humble. If you look at the universe with a pure heart, you, too, will see the face of God (cf. Mt 5:8), for it reveals the mystery of the Father's providential love.

Young people especially are sensitive to the beauty of nature and are spiritually inspired by contemplating it. But it needs to be authentic contemplation. Contemplation which fails to reveal the face of a personal, intelligent, free and loving Father, but which arrives only at the shadowy figure of an impersonal divinity or cosmic force, is not enough. We must not confuse the Creator with his creation.

The creature has no life of its own except from God. In discovering the greatness of God, man discovers the unique position which he occupies in the visible world: "You have made him little less than the angels, and crowned him with glory and honor. You have given him rule over the works of your hands, putting all things under his feet" (Ps 8:6-7). Yes, the contemplation of nature reveals not only the Creator but also the role of human beings in the world he has made. With faith, it reveals the greatness of our dignity as beings made in his image.

In order to have life and have it abundantly, in order to restore the original harmony of creation, we must respect that divine image in all of creation, and in a special way in human life itself.

7. *(In English)* When the light of faith penetrates this natural consciousness we reach a new certainty. The words of Christ ring out with utter truth: "I came that they might have life, and have it abundantly."

Against all the forces of death, in spite of all the false teachers, Jesus Christ continues to offer humanity the only true and realistic hope. He is the world's true Shepherd. This is because he and the Father are one (cf. Jn 17:22). In his divinity he is one with the Father; in his humanity he is one with us.

Because he took upon himself our human condition, Jesus Christ is able to communicate to all those who are united with him in baptism the life that he has in himself. And because in the Trinity, life is love, the very love of God has been poured out into our hearts through the Holy Spirit, who has been given to us (cf. Rom 5:5). Life and love are inseparable: the love of God for us, and the love we give in return—love of God and love of every brother and sister. This will be the theme of the last part of our reflection later this evening.

THIRD PART

Dear young pilgrims,

1. The Spirit has led you to Denver to fill you with new life: to give you a stronger faith and hope and love. Everything in you—your mind and heart, will and freedom, gifts and talents—everything is being taken up by the Holy Spirit in order to make you "living stones" of the "spiritual house" which is the Church (cf. 1 Pet 2:5). This Church is inseparable from Jesus; he loves her as the bridegroom loves the bride. This Church today, in the United States and in all the other countries from which you come, needs the affection and cooperation of her young people, the hope of her future. In the Church each one has a role to play, and all together we build up the one body of Christ, the one people of God.

As the third millennium approaches, the Church knows that the Good Shepherd continues, as always, to be the sure hope of humanity. Jesus Christ never ceases to be the "sheepgate." And despite the history of humanity's sins against life, he never ceases to repeat with the same vigor and love: "I came that they may have life, and have it abundantly" (Jn 10:10).

2. How is this possible? How can Christ give us life if death forms part of our earthly existence? How is it possible if "it is appointed that human beings die once, and after this the judgment" (Heb 9:27)?

Jesus himself provides the answer—and the answer is a supreme declaration of divine love, a high point of the Gospel revelation concerning God the Father's love for all of creation. The answer is already present in the parable of the Good Shepherd. Christ says: "The Good Shepherd lays down his life for the sheep" (Jn 10:11). Christ—the Good Shepherd—is present among us, among the peoples, nations, generations and races, as the one who "lays down his life for the sheep." What is this but the greatest love? It was the death of the Innocent One: "The Son of Man is departing, as Scripture says of him, but woe to that man by whom the Son of Man is betrayed" (Mt 26:24). Christ on the Cross stands as a sign of contradiction to every crime against the commandment not to kill. He offered his own life in sacrifice for the salvation of the world. No one takes that human life from him, but he lays it down of his own

> "Against all the forces of death, in spite of all the false teachers, Jesus Christ continues to offer humanity the only true and realistic hope. He is the world's true Shepherd. This is because he and the Father are one. In his divinity he is one with the Father; in his humanity he is one with us."

accord. He has the power to lay it down and the power to take it up again (cf. Jn 10:18). It was a true self-giving. It was a sublime act of freedom.

Yes, the Good Shepherd lays down his life. But only to take it up again (cf. Jn 10:17). And in the new life of the Resurrection, he has become—in the words of St. Paul—"a life-giving spirit" (1 Cor 15:45), who can now bestow the gift of life on all who believe in him.

Life laid down—life taken up again—life given. In him, we have that life which he has in the unity of the Father and of the Holy Spirit. If we believe in him. If we are one with him through love, remembering that "whoever loves God must also love his brother" (1 Jn 4:21).

3. (*In Spanish*) Good Shepherd, the Father loves you because you lay down your life. The Father loves you as the crucified one, because you go to death, giving your life for our sake. And the Father loves you when you overcome death through your Resurrection, revealing an indestructible life. You are the life—and as a result, the way and the truth of our lives (cf. Jn 14:6).

You said: "I am the Good Shepherd, and I know mine and mine know me, just as the Father knows me and I know the Father" (Jn 10:14-15). You who know the Father (cf. Jn 10:15)—the one common father of all—you know why the Father loves you (cf. Jn 10:17). He loves you because you offer your life for every one. When you say, "I give my life for the sheep," you leave no one out. You came into the world to embrace every individual, to gather into one the children of the entire human family who were scattered (cf. Jn 11:52). Yet, there are still many who do not know you: "I have other sheep that do not belong to this fold. I must lead them too" (Jn 10:16).

4. (*In English*) Good Shepherd, teach the young people gathered here, teach the young people of the world, the meaning of "laying down" their lives through vocation and mission. Just as you sent the apostles to preach the Gospel to the ends of the earth, so now challenge the youth of the Church to carry on the vast mission of making you known to all those who have not yet heard of you! Give these young people the courage and generosity of the great missionaries of the past so that, through the witness of their faith and their solidarity with every brother and sister in need, the world may discover the truth, the goodness and the beauty of the life you alone can give.

Teach the young people gathered in Denver to take your message of life and truth, of love and solidarity, to the heart of the modern metropolis—to the heart of all the problems which afflict the human family at the end of the twentieth century.

Teach these young people the proper use of their freedom. Teach them that the greatest freedom is the fullest giving of themselves. Teach them the meaning of the Gospel words: "He who loses his life for my sake will find it" (Mt 10:39).

5. For all of this, Good Shepherd, we love you.

The young people gathered in Denver love you because they love life, the gift of the Creator. They love their human life as the path through this created world. They love life as a task and a vocation.

And they love that other life which, through you, the eternal Father has given us: the Life of God in us, your greatest gift to us.

You are the Good Shepherd!

And there is none other.

You have come that we may have life—and that we may have it abundantly. Life, not only on the human level, but in the measure of the Son—the Son in whom the Father is eternally pleased.

Lord Jesus Christ, we thank you for having said: "I came that they may have life, and have it abundantly" (Jn 10:10). The young people of the eighth World Youth Day thank you from their hearts. Maranatha!

Here, from Cherry Creek State Park in Denver, from this gathering of young people from all over the world, we cry out:

Maranatha! "Come Lord Jesus" (Rev 22:20).

At Mass in Cherry Creek State Park
August 15

"God who is mighty has done great things for me" (Lk 1:49).

Beloved young people and dear friends in Christ,
1. Today the Church finds herself, with Mary, on the threshold of the house of Zechariah in Ain-Karim. With new life stirring within her, the Virgin of Nazareth hastened there, immediately after the fiat of the Annunciation, to be of help to her cousin Elizabeth. It was Elizabeth who first recognized the "great things" which God was doing in Mary. Filled with the Holy Spirit, Elizabeth marveled that the mother of her Lord should come to her (cf. Lk 1:43). With deep insight into the mystery, she declared: "Blest is she who believed that the Lord's words to her would be fulfilled" (Lk 1:45). With her soul full of humble gratitude to God, Mary replied with a hymn of praise: "God who is mighty has done great things for me and holy is his name" (Lk 1:49).

On this feast the Church celebrates the culmination of the "great things" which God has done in Mary: her glorious Assumption into heaven. And throughout the Church the same hymn of thanksgiving, the Magnificat, rings out as it did for the first time at Ain-Karim: All generations call you blessed (cf. Lk 1:48).

2. Gathered at the foot of the Rocky Mountains, which remind us that Jerusalem too was surrounded by hills (cf. Ps 124:2) and that Mary had gone up into those hills (cf. Lk 1:39), we are here to celebrate Mary's "going up" to the heavenly Jerusalem, to the threshold of the eternal temple of the Most Holy Trinity. Here in Denver, at the World Youth Day, the Catholic sons and daughters of America, together with others "from every tribe and tongue, people and nation" (Rev 5:9), join all the generations since who have cried out: God has done great things for you, Mary—and for all of us, members of his pilgrim people! (cf. Lk 1:49).

With my heart full of praise for the Queen of Heaven, the sign of hope and source of comfort on our pilgrimage of faith to "the heavenly Jerusalem" (Heb 12:22), I greet all of you who are present at this solemn liturgy. It is a pleasure for me to see so many priests, religious and lay faithful from Denver, from the State of Colorado, from all parts of the United States, and from so many countries of the world, who have joined the young people of the World Youth Day to honor the definitive victory of grace in Mary, the Mother of

the Redeemer.

The eighth World Youth Day is a celebration of life. This gathering has been the occasion of a serious reflection on the words of Jesus Christ: "I came that they may have life, and have it abundantly" (Jn 10:10). Young people from every corner of the world, in ardent prayer you have opened your hearts to the truth of Christ's promise of new life. Through the sacraments, especially penance and the Eucharist, and by means of the unity and friendship created among so many, you have had a real and transforming experience of the new life which only Christ can give. You, young pilgrims, have also shown that you understand that Christ's gift of life is not for you alone. You have become more conscious of your vocation and mission in the Church and in the world. For me, our meeting has been a deep and moving experience of your faith in Christ, and I make my own the words of St. Paul: "I have great confidence in you, I have great pride in you; I am filled with encouragement, I am overflowing with joy" (2 Cor 7:4).

These are not words of empty praise. I am confident that you have grasped the scale of the challenge that lies before you, and that you will have the wisdom and courage to meet that challenge. So much depends on you.

3. This marvelous world—so loved by the Father that he sent his only Son for its salvation (cf. Jn 3:17)—is the theater of a never-ending battle being waged for our dignity and identity as free, spiritual beings. This struggle parallels the apocalyptic combat described in the first reading of this Mass. Death battles against life: a "culture of death" seeks to impose itself on our desire to live, and live to the full. There are those who reject the light of life, preferring "the fruitless works of darkness" (Eph 5:11). Their harvest is injustice, discrimination, exploitation, deceit, violence. In every age, a measure of their apparent success is the death of the innocents. In our own century, as at no other time in history, the "culture of death" has assumed a social and institutional form of legality to justify the most horrible crimes against humanity: genocide, "final solutions," "ethnic cleansings" and the massive "taking of lives of human beings even before they are born, or before they reach the natural point of death" (cf. Dominum et vivificantem 57).

Today's reading from the Book of Revelation presents the woman surrounded by hostile forces. The absolute nature of their attack is symbolized in the object of their evil intention: the child, the symbol of new life. The "dragon" (Rev 12:3), the "ruler of this world" (Jn 12:31) and the "father of lies" (Jn 8:44), relentlessly tries to eradicate from human hearts the sense of gratitude and respect for the original, extraordinary and fundamental gift of God: human life itself. Today that struggle has become increasingly direct.

4. Dear friends, this gathering in Denver on the theme of life should lead us to a deeper awareness of the internal contradiction present in a part of the culture of the modern "metropolis."

When the founding fathers of this great nation enshrined certain inalienable rights in the Constitution—and something similar exists in many countries and in many international declarations—they did so because they recognized the existence of a "law"—a series of rights and duties—engraved by the Creator on each person's heart and conscience.

In much of contemporary thinking, any reference to a "law" guaranteed by the Creator is absent. There remains only each individual's choice of this or that objective as convenient or useful in a given set of circumstances. No longer is anything considered intrinsically "good" and "universally binding." Rights are affirmed but, because they are without any reference to an objective truth, they are deprived of any solid basis (cf. Congregation for the Doctrine of the Faith, "Threats to Human Life," I, iii). Vast sectors of society are confused about what is right and what is wrong and are at the mercy of those with the power to "create" opinion and impose it on others.

The family especially is under attack. And the sacred character of human life denied. Naturally, the weakest members of society are the most at risk: the unborn, children, the sick, the handicapped, the old, the poor and unemployed, the immigrant and refugee, the South of the world!

5. Young pilgrims, Christ needs you to enlighten the world and to show it the "path to life" (Ps 16:11). The challenge is to make the Church's Yes to life concrete and effective. The struggle will be long, and it needs each one of you. Place your intelligence, your talents, your enthusiasm, your compassion and your fortitude at the service of life!

Have no fear. The outcome of the battle for life is already decided, even though the struggle goes on against great odds and with much suffering. This certainty is what the second reading declares: "Christ is now raised from the dead, the first fruits of those who have fallen asleep...so in Christ all will come to life again" (1 Cor 15:20-22). The paradox of the Christian message is this: Christ—the Head—has already conquered sin and death. Christ in his body—the pilgrim people of God—continually suffers the onslaught of the Evil One and all the evil which sinful humanity is capable of.

6. At this stage of history, the liberating message of the Gospel of life has been put into your hands. And the mission of proclaiming it to the ends of the earth is now passing to your generation. Like the great Apostle Paul, you too must feel the full urgency of the task: "Woe to me if I do not evangelize" (1 Cor 9:16). Woe to you if you do not succeed in defending life. The Church needs your energies, your enthusiasm, your youthful ideals, in order to make the Gospel of life penetrate the fabric of society, transforming people's hearts and the structures of society in order to create a civilization of true justice and love. Now more than ever, in a world that is often without light and without the courage of noble ideals, people need the fresh, vital spirituality of the Gospel.

Do not be afraid to go out on the streets and into public places, like the first apostles who preached Christ and the good news of salvation in the squares of cities, towns and villages. This is no time to be ashamed of the Gospel (cf. Rom 1:16). It is the time to preach it from the rooftops (cf. Mt 10:27). Do not be afraid to break out of comfortable and routine modes of living, in order to take up the challenge of making Christ known in the modern "metropolis." It is you who must "go out into the byroads" (Mt 22:9) and invite everyone you meet to the banquet which God has prepared for his people. The Gospel must not be kept hidden because of fear or indifference. It was never meant to be hidden away in private. It has to be put on a stand so that people may see its light and give praise to our heavenly Father (cf. Mt 5:15-16).

Jesus went in search of the men and women of his time. He engaged them in an open and truthful dialogue, whatever their condition. As the Good Samaritan of the human family, he came close to people to heal them of their sins and of the wounds which life inflicts, and to bring them back to the Father's house. Young people

of World Youth Day, the Church asks you to go, in the power of the Holy Spirit, to those who are near and those who are far away. Share with them the freedom you have found in Christ. People thirst for genuine inner freedom. They yearn for the life which Christ came to give in abundance. The world at the approach of a new millennium, for which the whole Church is preparing, is like a field ready for the harvest. Christ needs laborers ready to work in his vineyard. May you, the Catholic young people of the world, not fail him. In your hands, carry the Cross of Christ. On your lips, the words of life. In your hearts, the saving grace of the Lord.

7. At her Assumption, Mary was "taken up to life"—body and soul. She is already a part of "the first fruits" (1 Cor 15:20) of our Savior's redemptive death and Resurrection. The Son took his human life from her; in return he gave her the fullness of communion in divine life. She is the only other being in whom the mystery has already been completely accomplished. In Mary the final victory of life over death is already a reality. And, as the Second Vatican Council teaches: "In the most holy Virgin the Church has already reached the perfection whereby she exists without spot or wrinkle" (Lumen gentium 65). In and through the Church we too have hope of "an inheritance which is imperishable, undefiled, and unfading, kept in heaven for us" (cf. 1 Pet 1:4).

You are blessed, O Mary! Mother of the Eternal Son born of your virgin womb, you are full of grace (cf. Lk 1:28). You have received the abundance of life (cf. Jn 10:10) as no one else among the descendants of Adam and Eve. As the most faithful "hearer of the Word" (cf. Lk 11:28), you not only treasured and pondered this mystery in your heart (cf. Lk 2:19, 51), but you observed it in your body and nourished it by the self-giving love with which you surrounded Jesus throughout his earthly life. As Mother of the Church, you guide us still from your place in heaven and intercede for us. You lead us to Christ, "the way, and the truth, and the life" (Jn 14:6), and help us to increase in holiness by conquering sin (cf. Lumen gentium 65).

8. The liturgy presents you, Mary, as the woman clothed with the sun (cf. Rev 12:1). But you are even more splendidly clothed with that divine light which can become the life of all those created in the image and likeness of God himself: "This life was the light of the human race; the light shines in the darkness, and the darkness has not overcome it" (Jn 1:4-5).

O woman clothed with the sun, the youth of the world greet you with so much love; they come to you with all the courage of their young hearts. Denver has helped them to become more conscious of the life which your divine Son has brought.

We are all witnesses of this.

These young people now know that life is more powerful than the forces of death; they know that the truth is more powerful than darkness; that love is stronger than death (cf. Song 6:8).

Your spirit rejoices, O Mary, and our spirit rejoices with you because the Mighty One has done great things for you and for us—for all these young people gathered here in Denver—and holy is his name!

His mercy is from age to age. We rejoice, Mary, we rejoice with you, Virgin assumed into heaven. The Lord has done great things for you! The Lord has done great things for us! Alleluia. Amen.

Angelus Talk at Cherry Creek State Park

August 15

I now invite all taking part in this concluding liturgy of the World Youth Day, and all who are in contact with us through radio and television, to turn in spirit to Mary, Mother of the Redeemer, and to join in reciting the Angelus prayer. This traditional prayer invites us to meditate on Mary's own pilgrimage of faith.

With trust we appeal to her: Mary, you are the "model of the Church in faith, charity and perfect union with Christ" (Lumen gentium 63). You freely accepted God's will, made known to you at the Annunciation. You bore in your womb the Word made flesh, who dwelt among us as your Son. You watched him grow "in wisdom and age and grace" (Lk 2:52) in the home of Nazareth. Your path of discipleship led even to the foot of the Cross, where Jesus made you the mother of all his followers (cf. Jn 19:27).

Mary, you are the Mother of the Lord of life who stood beneath the tree of life. At the Cross you became our spiritual mother and, from heaven, you continue to intercede for us who are still making our way toward the Father's house (cf. Lumen gentium 62).

Mary, Mother of the Church, in union with you we thank the blessed Trinity for all that this World Youth Day has accomplished in the lives of the young people who have followed the Holy Year Cross to Denver.

Mary, Immaculate Virgin, pray for these young people that they may "have life and have it to the full" (Jn 10:10). Accompany them as they go forth to be heralds of that divine life which alone can satisfy the hunger of the human heart! Like you, may they see in the Cross of Christ the call of divine love which turns death into life, despair into hope, and sadness into unending joy.

Blessed Mother, assist all the young people who are struggling to give a definitive and responsible Yes to the Lord's call to the priesthood, to the religious life or to a special consecration in the Church. Obtain for them the courage and hope they need to overcome all obstacles and to follow closely in the footsteps of your divine Son.

We ask you to watch over all of us gathered here as we continue our pilgrim way to the true source of life. For this pilgrimage must continue! It must continue in our lives. It must continue in the life of the Church as she looks toward the third Christian millennium. It must continue as "a new Advent," a time of hope and expectation, until the return of the Lord in glory. Our celebration of this World Youth Day has been a stop along the way, a moment of prayer and refreshment, but our journey must lead us on.

Today I wish to announce that the next World Youth Day will take place at the beginning of 1995 in Manila in the Philippines. In this way our pilgrimage will take us to the vast and vital continent of Asia. The Holy Year cross will lead us to a joyful meeting with the faithful, generous people of the Philippines.

Mary of the New Advent, we implore your protection on the preparations that will now begin for that next meeting.

Mary, "full of grace," we entrust the next World Youth Day to you!

Mary, assumed into heaven, we entrust the young people of the world to you!

Final Greetings at Cherry Creek State Park

August 15

The time has come for us to say goodbye, until we meet again. I wish to thank all those unnamed people, the members of the police, the fire department, the citizens of Denver, who have been our hosts and helpers during the World Youth Day.

I also mention Archbishop Stafford and all the volunteers of the Church here in Denver who have worked for months to prepare this day. Our gratitude goes to the local radio stations and the translators who have made it possible to follow the World Youth Day in the principal languages. To everyone in radio and television who are bringing World Youth Day to audiences in many countries.

My gratitude goes to Cardinal Pironio and the Pontifical Council for the Laity, who are responsible for organizing the World Youth Days at the international level.

To Archbishop Keeler, president of the bishops' conference, Monsignor Lynch and all their staff and all the bishops for their cooperation: thanks to the whole Church in the United States. A special thanks to all the cardinals and bishops who have become pilgrims together with their young people from all the continents. The World Youth Day has been a great event, and there has been a wonderful exchange of spiritual gifts and experiences between all the young people present. For all of this we must give praise and thanks to God.

I wish to express my deep and warm appreciation to the representatives of the other Christian churches and communities, as well as to the representatives of the various religious traditions, who have taken such an active part in World Youth Day.

(In Spanish) How can I not thank all the Spanish-speaking Catholics of the United States for the many young people present at this meeting! My thanks also go to all who have come from Mexico, from Central and South America and from Spain. May God be praised for your faith, your generosity and your desire to live the life Christ gives you. Bring the heartfelt greeting of the pope to your families, your friends and to the nations and peoples from which you have come.

(In Italian) The moment of departure leads us to say: arrivederci a Roma! Dear Italian young people, take with you the interior experience of the new life which only Christ can give. Let that life become in you the seed of important works of ecclesial life and of renewal in the life of society. Preserve the enthusiasm of these days, with full trust in Christ, in Mary, in the Church.

(In French) To all the French-speaking pilgrims, I say goodbye, with an immense hope that the experience of Denver will lead to many new initiatives in the task of announcing the Gospel to the youth of your respective countries. God bless you all! May the Holy Spirit continue his work in you! God bless you and keep you!

(In German) I am happy that a large group of German-speaking pilgrims was able to come to Denver. Now, as you return home and take up the challenges of your daily life, keep in mind the insights gained in these days. Above all remember that Christ is the true source of life, and joy and happiness. Share this conviction with your contemporaries. Work to build a civilization of respect for every human being. With Christ's grace, be witnesses of the good news of salvation.

(In Portuguese) To the Portuguese-speaking young people, in

saying goodbye, I wish to encourage you to become ever more effective apostles and missionaries of the word of Christ in the Gospel. I hope that you will carry with you the joy of a new commitment to the Church and the human development of your brothers and sisters. Praised be Jesus Christ!

(In Polish) The Virgin of Jasna Gora is the virgin of the "new Advent." We are in the time of preparation for the millennium jubilee of the birth of our Redeemer. This must be a period of commitment so that the Church can count on your youthful energies in meeting the challenges of changes in culture and in society which do not always reflect the truth about man and his destiny.

In Denver you have reflected on the promise of Christ to give life and give it abundantly (cf. Jn 10:10). Have confidence in him! Have confidence in yourselves too. You have a mission, and God's grace will sustain you.

(In Russian) May God strengthen and protect you as you return to your homes. Take my greetings to your families and friends. God bless your country and all its citizens.

(In Lithuanian) Until we meet in September! Tell your friends how much the pope looks forward to that visit. May the Mother of Wisdom guide you on the great pilgrimage of life!

(In Croatian) The theme of the World Youth Day is especially significant for you and the people of the Balkans. Let us invoke God's blessings of peace upon the whole region. The noise of battle and the specter of death and suffering must give way to the joy of peace and harmony among peoples. You must face great challenges. Be assured of the prayers of the pope and of the Church.

(In Arabic) God's peace be with you all! May you grow as witnesses of Christ!

(In Tagalog) Our next step on our pilgrimage will be Manila in 1995. I hope that the young people of the Philippines will prepare spiritually for that occasion. May they be encouraged and strengthened by the particular devotion of their nation to the blessed Mother of God. She indicates the path: your generosity will give reality to her maternal wishes for the Church in your land.

(In Swahili) God bless you all with faith and hope and love.

(In Korean) May you grow into the maturity which Christ expects of his followers, and be apostles of his word and mission to the world.

(In Vietnamese) Mary, the Mother of Christ, shows you the path of discipleship. It is not an easy path, but your confidence is in Christ who loves you and never abandons his faithful people. God bless you! God bless your fatherland!

Farewell at Stapleton Airport
August 15

Dear Mr. Vice President,
Dear friends,
Dear people of America,
1. As I take my leave of the United States, I express my gratitude to you, Mr. Vice President, who are here to say goodbye, and to President Clinton, who kindly welcomed me on my arrival, for the courtesy I have received at every stage of this visit.

I wish to thank all those who in any way have cooperated in ensuring the success of this eighth World Youth Day, which has brought young pilgrims from almost every country in the world to the beautiful city of Denver, to reflect on the words of Jesus Christ: "I came that they might have life, and have it abundantly" (Jn 10:10).

2. I too came as a pilgrim, a pilgrim of hope. I have always known that for the Church and for civil society young people constitute the hope of our future. But over the years of my ministry, especially through the celebration of events such as this one, that hope has been confirmed and strengthened again and again. It has been the young people themselves who have taught me to have ever new and ever greater confidence. It is not just that the young people of today are the adults of the future who will step into our shoes and carry on the human adventure. No, the longing present in every heart for a full and free life that is worthy of the human person is particularly strong in them. Certainly, false answers to this longing abound, and humanity is far from being a happy and harmonious family. But so many young people in all societies refuse to descend into selfishness and superficiality. They refuse to relinquish responsibility. That refusal is a beacon of hope.

For believers, commitment to the spiritual and moral renewal which society needs is a gift of the Spirit of the Lord who fills the whole earth, for it is the Spirit who offers man the light and the strength to measure up to his supreme destiny (cf. Gaudium et spes 10). This has been particularly evident in the prayer-filled attitude of the young people gathered here. As a result, they go away more committed to the victory of the culture of life over the culture of death. The culture of life means respect for nature and protection of God's work of creation. In a special way it means respect for human life from the first moment of conception until its natural end. A genuine culture of life is all the more essential when—as I have written in the social encyclical Centesimus annus—"human ingenuity seems to be directed more toward limiting, suppressing or destroying the sources of life—including recourse to abortion, which unfortunately is so widespread in the world—than toward defending and opening up the possibilities of life" (no. 39).

A culture of life means service to the underprivileged, the poor and the oppressed, because justice and freedom are inseparable and exist only if they exist for everyone. The culture of life means thanking God every day for his gift of life, for our worth and dignity as human beings, and for the friendship and fellowship he offers us as we make our pilgrim way toward our eternal destiny.

3. Mr. Vice President, I leave the United States with gratitude to God in my heart. Gratitude for what has happened here in the World Youth Day. Gratitude to the American people for being open and generous and for the many ways in which they continue to assist needy people around the world. I pray that America will continue to believe in its own noble ideals, and I express the hope that the United States will be a wise and helpful partner in the multilateral efforts being made to resolve some of the more difficult questions facing the international community.

My gratitude becomes an ardent prayer for the people of this great country, for the fulfillment of America's destiny as one nation under God, with liberty and justice for all.

America, defend life so that you may live in peace and harmony.

God bless America!
God bless you all!

PHOTOGRAPHIC CREDITS

(BY PAGE NUMBER)

Photos provided by Catholic News Service

Joanne Asher 65, 94, 104

Blimp Photo Company 45

Karen Callaway 42

Michael Edrington 53, 54, 55, 56, 57, 64, 66-67, 69, 82, 84, 86, 87, 88, 89 (two), 90, 92,93

Grzegorz Galazka 40

Jack Hamilton 43

Amy Hollst 58

W. H. Keeler 105

Lisa Kessler 48-49

KNA 10, 33, 38

Arturo Mari 8, 16, 17, 18, 19, 20-21, 22, 24, 26, 27, 29, 30, 31, 32, 34-35, 36, 79

Polish Interpress Agency 11, 12, 13, 14

Joe Rimkus, Jr. 15, 50, 52, 59, 60, 61, 70, 72, 73, 74, 75, 76-77, 78, 80-81, 81 (top right), 95, 96-97, 98, 99, 102, 106-107, 109, 110, 111

Charles Schisla 46, 62, 66 (top left), 107 (top right), 108

Joan Smithwick 47

Vatican Press Office 85 (bottom)

Nancy Wiechec 68, 85 (top left), 100, 101

Mark Zimmermann 63